Ireland and the Ryder Cup

Ireland and the Ryder Cup

Paul Kelly

Gill & Macmillan

To W.

Gill & Macmillan Ltd
Hume Avenue, Park West, Dublin 12
with associated companies throughout the world
www.gillmacmillan.ie
© Paul Kelly 2006
ISBN-13: 978 07171 4015 2
ISBN-10: 0 7171 4015 6
Index compiled by Cover to Cover
Design and print origination by Designit
Colour reproduction by Typeform Repro, Dublin
Printed by Butler & Tanner, Frome

This book is typeset in Palatino 9.5pt on 14pt.

The paper used in this book comes from the wood pulp of managed forests. For every tree felled, at least one tree is planted, thereby renewing natural resources.

A CIP catalogue record for this book is available from the British Library.

5 4 3 2 1

Picture Credits

For permission to reproduce photographs the author and publisher gratefully acknowledge the following:

162, 175 © Action Images; 10, 21, 22, 36, 40, 44, 68, 95, 99, 102, 116, 118, 124, 125, 136, 146, 166, 187, 188, 191 © Alamy/ Popperfoto; Corbis: 12 © Bettmann, 27 © Hulton-Deutsch Collection, 160 © Tempsport, 158 © Tony Roberts; 112 © The Irish Times; 7B, 20, 24, 50, 58, 64, 70, 74, 86, 88, 100, 126, 139, 192, 231 © EMPICS; Getty Images: 140, 170, 176, 179, 180, 210, 219 © Getty, 7T, 216 © AFP, 8, 29, 31, 47, 67, 82, 104 © Hulton Archive; 9, 38, 43, 121, 122, 129, 132, 135, 165, 172, 182, 184, 194, 196, 198, 199, 200, 201, 202, 205, 206, 208, 213, 214, 217, 220, 222, 224, 227, 228, 232, 235 © Inpho; 62, 90 © Pacemaker Press International; 96, 111 © Phil Sheldon Golf Picture Library; 52, 61, 73, 76, 85, 92, 107, 143 © Popperfoto.com; 108, 130, 144, 153, 154, 156 © Sportsfile.com; 15, 16, 19, 26, 28, 33, 34, 39, 46, 48, 55, 56, 78, 81, 149, 150, 169 © Topfoto

The author and publisher have made every effort to trace all copyright holders, but if any has been inadvertently overlooked we would be pleased to make the necessary arrangement at the first opportunity.

Contents

Acknowledgments 6

Introduction 7

1. Fred Daly 10

2. Harry Bradshaw 22

3. Christy O'Connor 36

4. Norman Drew 50

5. Jimmy Martin 64

6. Hugh Boyle 76

7. Eddie Polland 90

8. John O'Leary 102

9. Christy O'Connor Junior 116

10. Eamonn Darcy 130

11 Des Smyth 144

12 Ronan Rafferty 158

13 David Feherty 170

14 Philip Walton 182

15 Darren Clarke 194

16 Padraig Harrington 208

17 Paul McGinley 222

Appendix 1 Players and Records 236

Appendix 2 Ryder Cup Teams 236

Select Bibliography 237

Index 238

Acknowledgments

There are many people who provided invaluable help and direction during the period when I was researching and then writing this book.

During those times when it felt like I was getting nowhere fast, I received a lot of encouragement and support from my family and my friends. In many ways their enthusiasm for the project often seemed greater than my own and it sustained me during the periods when things weren't going to plan.

To anyone who ever asked me how things were going with 'the book' I would like to say a big thank you. It meant a lot to know that people were interested in how the project was progressing.

I would not of course have got very far without the co-operation of many of the golfers who appear in the book.

I set out to record the experiences of Ireland's representatives in the Ryder Cup. At the back of it all I remain first and foremost a fan and it was a thrill for me to meet and speak to each and every one of them.

To Norman Drew, Eddie Polland, John O'Leary, Hugh Boyle, David Feherty, Paul McGinley, Christy O'Connor Jnr, Christy O'Connor Snr, Des Smyth and Padraig Harrington I'd like to offer a special word of thanks for taking the time to discuss their Ryder Cup experiences with me.

I couldn't have made contact with the golfers without the help of a string of people who worked in the background to set up interviews and meetings.

Many thanks go to Roddy Williams and all at the European Tour Media Department, Martin Hardy at ISM, Adrian Mitchell at IMG, Barry Tjersen at Tour Talent, Roe McCroffin, Declan O'Donaghue, Michael McCumiskey of the Irish PGA and all at the Buckinghamshire Golf Club.

I'd also like to take this opportunity to offer my sincere thanks to a number of media professionals who provided some interesting insights into the Ryder Cup.

Jack Magowan of the *Belfast Telegraph* was a mine of information about Ireland's only Open Championship winner, Fred Daly, while Dermot Gilleece of the *Irish Independent* pointed me in the right direction on Jimmy Martin.

The renowned television commentator Peter Alliss spoke eloquently about the impact Irish golfers have had on the Ryder Cup, while Tony Adamson, formerly BBC Radio golf correspondent and a man with Co. Donegal roots, revealed his great passion for the event.

To Fergal Tobin at Gill & Macmillan, thanks for taking a chance and thanks also to Helen Thompson who sourced the pictures and Deirdre Rennison Kunz in editorial.

Finally, a number of people are worthy of special mention: Nicky Lynch, professional at Sutton Golf Club who spoke with genuine warmth about his friend, the late Jimmy Martin; Michelle Donnelly, who provided me with accommodation during an overnight stay in London; and to my dad, Brian Kelly, who was badgered and cajoled into proofing the various drafts I served up.

Introduction

In August 2004, as the battle for places on the European Ryder Cup team reached a thrilling conclusion, Thomas Bjorn was asked about the wildcard headache facing captain Bernhard Langer.

The Danish golfer, a two time Ryder Cup player who would later act as one of Langer's on-course assistants at Oakland Hills, had no hesitation in promoting the claims of Paul McGinley.

The Dubliner, hero of the 2002 Ryder Cup at the Belfry, was nearing the end of a marathon nine-week playing stretch as he sought to force his way on to the team which would defend the title in America.

'Paul McGinley is the key factor in the whole Ryder Cup team make-up,' said Bjorn.

'He's the guy who is playing the best and he's done really well to get where he is on the table and Bernhard

Padraig Harrington and Paul McGinley celebrate with Irish fans after beating Tiger Woods and Davis Love III during the Ryder Cup at Oakland Hills (September 2004).

Samuel Ryder, a seed merchant, developed a passion for golf and commissioned the trophy for which the teams compete.

should remember that. You also have to remember that Paul is Irish and the Irish seem to win Ryder Cups.'

Statistically speaking, there is some merit in Thomas's theory. In the 59 years since Fred Daly became the first Irish Ryder Cup player, an Irish golfer has been part of a winning side six times, in 1957, 87, 95, 97, 2002 and 2004.

Of those six wins, an Irishman has holed the winning putt three times. That's a remarkable strike rate when you consider the many variables that are involved in getting an Irish golfer in the right place at the right time to hole the winning putt in the Ryder Cup. And before you say that it's a poor return, just remember that in the 59 years since Fred first played, GB & I and latterly Europe have won the Ryder Cup a mere seven times (there have been two halved matches, in 1969 and 1989).

It's unlikely, however, that before Thomas made his statement he had taken the time to go through the records. What he was referring to had little to do with number-crunching; it even had little to do with the actual winning or losing of matches.

What he was alluding to is something which has far more to do with basic gut instinct — in the heat of a Ryder Cup battle an Irishman will never let you down.

It's an understanding borne out of the deeds of Ireland's great triumvirate, Fred Daly, Harry Bradshaw and Christy O'Connor. Through their exploits and those of renowned amateurs Joe Carr and Jimmy Bruen, the image of Irish golfers as tenacious, shot-making match play exponents was spread across the world. Ireland's golfing trailblazers never shirked a challenge and rarely turned down a match.

More importantly, in the context of the Ryder Cup, they were excellent team men.

'The Irish golfers bought into the team ethos and they helped enormously with team spirit in all the Ryder Cups I played on,' said renowned golf commentator Peter Alliss.

'They were very good on the course and in the dressing room. In many ways they were all typically Irish. They had a way of saying and phrasing things that kept the pot boiling and kept the tension levels down. They engendered a spirit of togetherness, wanting everyone to play well, and they were always encouraging the team to go out and try their best.'

This willingness to buy into the idea of team competition certainly went a long way towards developing the image of Irishmen as key components in a successful team, but it also went some way to covering up deficiencies on the course.

Irish golfers suffered with the rest of their Ryder Cup team mates during the dark days of the 1950s, 60s and 70s. The reality is that even Ireland's greatest Ryder Cup player, Christy O'Connor, lost more than he won. In ten Ryder Cup appearances Christy played 36 times, winning only 11 matches.

The GB & I teams at the time were simply too weak to cope with their US opponents and all the encouragement and tactful Irish advice in the world can't help you when you are simply outclassed.

Yet, while Christy's record and those of his Irish contemporaries may not be great, their competitive approach left a lasting impression on their team mates and their opponents.

'If the weather was bad there was an expectation that the Irish golfers would play well,' added Alliss.

'It was the same for both the professionals and the amateurs. Look at the great Joe Carr and the number of championships he won. Christy and Fred Daly played so much golf by the seaside and in the early days a lot of golf was played at championship links courses, so when the wind blew and whenever there was some dirty weather about, there was this feeling — perhaps it was a slight myth — that the Irish players were more used to it.'

Rightly or wrongly, the feeling persists that Irish golfers excel at the match play form of the game. It's an image that has only grown stronger in recent years with Irish golfers playing a key role in Europe's success.

Spectators used 'periscopes' to watch the action at the Ryder Cup at Royal Birkdale (October 1965).

Christy O'Connor *(fourth from left)* **pictured with the GB & I Ryder Cup team ahead of the event at Royal Birkdale (October 1969).**

'I can't work out what there is about the Irish psyche that makes them such good match play exponents,' said Tony Adamson, BBC Radio's voice of golf for over 25 years.

Adamson, a native of Donegal, has watched Irish golfers like Eamonn Darcy, Philip Walton and Paul McGinley tip the balance of power from America back towards Europe over the last decade.

'I think you need to be careful that you don't analyse these things too much, but they (Irish golfers) definitely have an ability to keep calm and cool in the pressurised situation,' said Tony.

'I get the impression that the Irish players find relaxing in a tight situation a little easier. I mean, take Paul McGinley, who has been known not to relax. When the biggest moment of his golfing career came along, he looked unbelievably calm at the Belfry; and the same thing happened with Philip Walton in 1995 at Oak Hill when he won. There was a sort of serenity that came over him that day that I had never seen in Philip before. I think they are inspired by the Ryder Cup and they somehow manage to keep that inspiration inside working for them.'

In Tony's mind that inspiration comes from the team environment, but increasingly he also feels the supporters have helped pull the Irish players through in difficult situations.

'I think that's a huge plus. I really do. It happened in America at Oakland Hills and it also happened at the Belfry,' added Tony.

'The Irish contingent in the crowd have been fantastic and I think that has been a huge plus for the Irish players. I think they take more from the crowd and the Irish supporters than some of the other players do. When Harrington and McGinley played together in 2004 (against Tiger Woods and Davis Love) they desperately wanted to be close to the Irish support, and I think that kind of approach and attitude helps their golf.

'It's not just the two of them; it's hundreds of people and there's a togetherness about them that you really only find in Ireland. There is a closeness and a camaraderie that is massive.

'You would think that in some way when they are standing over pressurised putts like McGinley was, it would act against them; but in fact he's leading a clan and he wants to hole it for them, for his country, not just for himself, and I think that's inspirational.'

Seventeen Irish golfers have played in the Ryder Cup since Fred Daly pulled on that GB & I blazer for the first time back in 1947. In many ways Ireland has punched above its weight in that time, but that speaks volumes for the character of the men who have competed in the event.

Ireland and Irish golfers have left an indelible impression on the Ryder Cup, and that looks set to continue in 2006 when the event finally comes to these shores at the K Club in September.

Chapter 1

Fred Daly

Fred Daly holes a putt to win his Ryder Cup foursomes match at Wentworth (1953).

In the beginning there was Fred Daly.

Before Bradshaw and O'Connor, Fred Daly ensured that Irish golfers would be counted among the world's elite. He did so by never shirking a challenge and along with amateurs Joe Carr and Jimmy Bruen, he cemented the reputation of Irish golfers as fierce competitors.

'Daly was the finest competitor of his day after Cotton,' wrote *Observer* journalist Pat Ward Thomas.

'There was steel in the man, and in match play especially, he was capable of playing unanswerable golf.'

Fred Daly admires the Ryder Cup trophy at the dinner given in honour of the visiting GB & I team by Robert A. Hudson at the Waldorf Astoria, New York (1947).

Fred secured his place among the legends of Irish sport by winning the Open Championship in 1947 at Hoylake. He played in four consecutive Ryder Cups from 1947 to 1953, won the British match play title three times and claimed the Ulster Professional title a record 11 times.

Belfast Telegraph journalist Jack Magowan, a friend of Daly for over 25 years, claims that during that six-year period Fred became something of a national treasure.

He elevated Irish golf to a new level and he did so without ever losing his warmth, loyalty and sense of humour.

● ● ● ●

Fred was the son of a blacksmith, born in 1911 and raised in Portrush. His love affair with the game started as a caddie on the famous links earning the measly sum of ninepence.

'If I was lucky I got a thrupenny tip. If not, then I made sure the old codger who didn't tip lost a ball or two and later went out and found them myself,' he said.

Fred honed his game at Portrush, repeatedly hitting balls from what is now the car park towards the first green. It was there, on the tight links fairways, that he developed and mastered his control of long iron play. It was regularly said that he could knock the hat off your head from 200 yards and the great Sam Snead referred to him as the 'prince of long iron players'.

Fred was 19 when he turned professional and took a job as club pro at Mahee Island in County Down. He had to serve a three-year apprenticeship with the club before he could earn a penny from tournaments. During the

'Well, Fred came over and told me the club wasn't for me. "You need this one," he said, handing me a club. He gave me a 16 pound hammer. When I got it up to the top of my backswing I couldn't get it back down again! It was one of his own and had extra weight in it.'

From Mahee Island, Fred moved to the City of Derry Club, then to Lurgan and finally to Balmoral Golf Club in Belfast. Balmoral would be Fred's home for the remainder of his career. Along with his wife Jean he settled into life in the city and raised a family. He did so against the backdrop of the Second World War, a period when golf naturally took a back seat.

Fred was 28 and just reaching his prime when war broke out, and who knows what he might have achieved had

'Peter Alliss commented that Daly's clubs were made for Goliath and he was mystified as to how Fred swung them at all.'

winter he would sign on the dole for 25 shillings a week and he kept fit by playing badminton and hockey.

'Fred was small and quite wiry, but he was very strong,' added Jack.

'In his prime he weighed just 10 stone but his strong wrists and a large shoulder turn allowed him to hit the ball a long way. It was remarkable, considering he used some of the heaviest clubs of the era.

'Peter Alliss commented that Daly's clubs were made for Goliath and he was mystified as to how Fred swung them at all.

'I remember I was in the shop one day chatting to him and I was looking around at a few clubs. I liked the look of one, picked it up and had a couple of practice swings.

war not intervened. When hostilities ceased, he wasted no time in making his presence felt. He was in his middle thirties and he was determined to make up for lost time.

Victory at Hoylake ensured that Daly would be selected for the Ryder Cup team bound for Portland, Oregon, but it was his triumph a few months later in the British Match Play Championship at Lytham and St Anne's which marked him down as something of a match play expert.

'Fred was absolute mustard at match play. He was a cold, thinking golfer who played the course, rarely worrying about his opponent,' said Jack Magowan. This assessment was shared by Gerald Micklem, a past captain of the R & A, who used to talk about Fred's secret weapon, his 'ice-cold temperament'.

On his way to winning that first match play title, the Ulsterman put one over on Henry Cotton, a man who held Fred in high regard. In Cotton's mind, winning the Open was the pinnacle of professional golf, and for that reason alone he put Daly ahead of his Irish contemporaries.

The two men met in the semifinal at Lytham and St Anne's. Leaving the 14th Fred was two up.

'The 15th at Lytham was in those days a par five of nearly 460 yards,' recalled Fred some years later.

'We both hit good drives with Henry just a fraction longer than me. With the wind blowing across the hole, the second shot was still a wood, but I decided to try a bluff. I told my caddie loudly enough for everyone to hear that I was going to use my old cleek and then proceeded to slam a shot under the wind straight at the flag. It was one of the best shots I ever hit in a

'Confidence and a cool head are a golfer's best allies, and I always went into a match feeling I could win,' he said.

Fred took that same confidence into his first encounter with the Americans in November 1947. 'The trophy's already on the ship,' he claimed as the GB & I team arrived in America. Unfortunately Fred's confidence was misplaced as the Americans swept aside their opponents by an 11-1 margin at the rain-sodden Portland Golf Club.

In the 36-hole foursomes Fred was partnered with Charlie Ward against Lloyd Mangrum and Sam Snead. The US pairing led six up at the interval and went on to win comfortably by 6 and 5.

In the 36-hole singles Fred, as befitted the British match play champion, was out first against Dutch Harrison who replaced the United States captain Ben Hogan.

> ## 'The trophy's already on the ship,' he claimed as the GB & I team arrived in America.

tournament, but I didn't know if it was home, and neither did Henry.

'I was sure of this much, however. The maestro wouldn't stoop to hitting a wooden club after I had hit an iron; and if I couldn't make it with an iron, he certainly couldn't.'

The bluff worked. Cotton took a two-iron, tried to get too much distance on it and pulled the shot off line eventually conceding the hole to Daly's birdie. Fred was three up with three to play and went on to claim the title, thus proving to the world that his Open victory wasn't a fluke.

Fred played poorly over the opening nine holes to trail by three and despite winning the 6th he found himself five down after 18. It gave him little room for manoeuvre and he eventually slumped to a 5 and 4 defeat.

Chastened by the experience, he later declared: 'I learned one thing in America. The hole will never come to the ball.'

In hindsight it's not surprising that the GB & I team were so heavily defeated. Fred's natural ebullience failed to cover up the yawning gap between the sides. On a most basic level the US team were better prepared for the contest. Their top players had continued to play

Having won his Ryder Cup singles match against Ted Kroll, Fred Daly is congratulated by *(left to right)*
Mrs Charlie Ward, wife of the golfer, Mrs Alice May and Mrs Lloyd Mangrum, wife of America's team captain (1953).

competitively during the war while golf in Europe had effectively ceased during the same period.

The GB & I team, with rationing still in force, were physically not as strong as their opponents. They had also endured an arduous sea journey followed by a three and a half day rail trip to reach Portland.

Whilst Fred clearly didn't do himself justice, the heavy defeat failed to dampen his enthusiasm for the Ryder Cup.

'He loved it. You must remember, in those days there was no tour as we know it now. There was a maximum of six to eight tournaments a year, so for players like

Fred the Ryder Cup was a welcome opportunity to play top-class competitive golf,' said Jack Magowan.

'When the GB & I boys travelled to America they marvelled at the facilities the Americans had at their disposal. The Americans worked harder at their game, practised harder and, more importantly, had the time to do so.

'Fred, like many of the top-class professionals of the day over here, had a shop and club members to attend to. If he wanted to go and play in an event, he had to find someone to run the shop, otherwise there was simply no money coming in.'

Fred Daly pictured with other members of the GB & I Ryder Cup team, drives off the golf deck aboard the *Queen Mary* **(1947).**

Jack also feels that the GB & I players struggled to get over that 'wow' factor when faced with the likes of Sam Snead or Ben Hogan.

'Even Fred, early on in his Ryder Cup career, felt that sense of awe when pitted against the "greats" of the day,' added Jack.

'Fred saw Hogan as the embodiment of the modern professional golfer. His flawless long iron striking was an obvious comparison between the two men, but Fred was also impressed by Hogan's winning mentality.'

Fred may well have marvelled at the Americans on his debut, but by the time the Americans returned to Ganton, Yorkshire, for the 1949 matches, any sense of deference was quickly dispelled. The GB & I team jumped into a 3-1 lead at the end of day one with Daly,

regain the trophy. The team needed 3½ points and Fred, full of confidence, was put out last in the eight singles matches by captain Charlie Whitcombe.

Fred found himself lining up against the man who beat him so comprehensively on his foursomes debut at Portland, Lloyd Mangrum. Ever the competitor, Fred wouldn't have needed any further incentive and the two men traded birdies from the start in what is now recognised as one of the great Ryder Cup matches.

It was a tie that severely tested Gerald Micklem's assertion that he had 'never seen Fred push the panic button'.

Mangrum's opening round of 65 would ordinarily have been enough to secure a healthy lead, but the American went in for lunch leading by just a single hole as Daly,

> **'Even Fred, early on in his Ryder Cup career, felt that sense of awe when pitted against the "greats" of the day.'**

partnering Ken Bousfield, claiming his first Ryder Cup point in the opening day foursomes.

The victory was built on a sparkling opening nine holes from the GB & I pair who went to the turn in 33 shots. Their opponents, Skip Alexander and Bob Hamilton, fought back over the back nine to level matters but lost the 17th and 18th to give Daly and Bousfield a two-hole lead at lunch.

That lead was soon extended in the afternoon and a wonderful bunker shot from Bousfield at the 14th eventually sealed the points as the GB & I pairing ran out 4 and 2 winners.

After the humiliation at Portland, there was real hope among the fans and the media that the home side could

showing all his famous fighting qualities, fired an opening round 66 which included a brave 17 foot putt to win the 18th.

Daly started the back nine well, winning two of the opening three holes to lead for the first time, but Mangrum responded by taking the lead again before Daly levelled things with a two at the 168 yard par three 10th. It was going to take something remarkable to separate the two men, and it was Mangrum who found that extra edge, remarkably finishing 12 under par for 33 holes to win a vital point for the visitors.

'When Mangrum hit me with everything but his driver, I still felt I could get him in the end. I didn't, but I felt I could. It was the finest game that I never won,' said Fred later.

Fred's never say die attitude was in evidence again two years later at Pinehurst during his singles match with Clayton Heafner. Having endured an opening day foursomes defeat at the hands of Ben Hogan and Jimmy Demaret, Fred was in no mood to leave America without something to show for his efforts.

However, a fourth consecutive defeat on US soil looked likely when Heafner opened with a 70 to grab a three-hole lead at lunch which the American then clung on to in the afternoon to be three up with three to play. Fred refused to be beaten and birdied the par five 16th and the par three 17th to cut Heafner's lead to just one up with only the 18th left to play.

'I always liked people. The bigger the gallery and the occasion, the better I usually played.'

This unrelenting approach to match play was perfectly illustrated during his Ryder Cup swansong in the 1953 matches at Wentworth. Playing for Henry Cotton, a captain whom he admired and respected, and in front of a large home crowd, the 42-year-old Ulsterman took Ted Kroll apart in the 36-hole singles.

Fred shot an immaculate 32 over the opening nine holes and Kroll found himself six down.

The two men found the fairway, but Heafner dumped his approach into the greenside bunker and Fred, with another unerring iron, found the middle of the green to set up his third win in a row and secure a remarkable half for GB & I who sadly slumped to another heavy defeat.

'There was something dauntless and heroic about Daly's golf in those days,' added Jack Magowan.

'He was a scrapper, loved being in the thick of it, but played with a smile on his face. He used to whistle away between shots. It was his way of remaining relaxed and loose. At his best he was absolutely ruthless.'

Fred's explanation for his whistling was simple. 'Golf is one game in which you can't afford to get uptight. Lose your cool and you lose concentration, tempo, swing and everything else that blends to make a good score,' he said.

Fred shot an immaculate 32 over the opening nine holes and Kroll found himself six down at lunch after the first 18 holes. The American fared no better in the afternoon as Fred blitzed his hapless opponent on his way to completing a stunning 9 and 7 victory. It was the largest winning margin in 20 years and the third largest margin by a GB & I player.

'That was some ball game. I had gone round the Burma Road course in 66 for a six-hole lead and just couldn't do a thing wrong. It was one of those days. If I'd played with an umbrella and a bloody orange I'd still have won,' recalled Fred.

The performance was all the more remarkable when you consider that Fred had been having a poor year by his standards, particularly on the greens. Maybe the

Fred Daly is cheered by well-wishers after winning the Open Championship at Hoylake (July 1947).

fact that fellow Irishman Harry Bradshaw, a close friend, was also on the team helped to inspire him. The two men had combined on the opening day to save GB & I from a foursomes whitewash, with Fred holing a four yard putt on the last despite declaring midway through the morning round, 'My putting's away to hell, Harry. I'll put it on the green; you put it in the hole.'

Cotton had put the two men out last against the rookie US pairing of Walter Burkemo and Cary Middlecroft.

Fred Daly drives from the 1st tee at St Andrews (May 1949).

The Americans found themselves three down at lunch and despite an early afternoon fight back, they were still three down with nine holes left to play.

Burkemo, in his only Ryder Cup appearance, then launched a one-man rearguard action that reduced the gap to just one hole with two to play. Middlecroft missed a seven-footer to level the match at the 17th and then failed to convert a birdie putt at the 18th which would have secured a half for the Americans. Fred was left with his 10 foot putt to win the point and after surveying it from all angles he rolled the ball

forward and into the cup, sparking huge roars from the crowd.

The Times, reporting on the opening day, stated: 'Only once could British lungs really let themselves go and that was when Daly, architect of victory in the bottom match, holed a long putt on the last green to give the British team its only win.'

Bradshaw stated simply some years later: 'He (Daly) was indeed a great golfer and had nerves of steel when the crunch came.'

Despite the sterling work of the Irish contingent, who finished the event with a 100 per cent record, the cup remained in US hands following a late collapse in the singles by rookies Peter Alliss and Bernard Hunt.

Fred, like many golfers throughout that era, never tasted Ryder Cup victory. His game never again reached the heights of those two days in early October and he gradually reduced his tournament appearances, spending more time at Balmoral. In the early 1980s he was awarded what many thought was an 'overdue'

sleep." He would always say, "Awwh, we will Jack." And we always did.

'I would say, "For God's sake sleep on your side", but as soon as his head hit the pillow he was off and snoring. On one occasion it got so bad that I went down to the bar, got one of those plastic drinks bottles, filled it with water and put it behind him to try and stop him from rolling over. It didn't make any difference. He just rolled over and slept on the bottle!'

'He was indeed a great golfer and had nerves of steel when the crunch came.'

MBE and he finally passed away in November 1990 at the age of 79.

'Fred remained an integral feature of Irish golf long after he retired. He was a generous, modest man who loved company and had an opinion on any subject,' said Jack Magowan.

'I used to take him down to the annual Golf Writers' dinner in Dublin. I often used to say to my wife, "I hope Fred's not invited this year." You see, we always ended up sharing the same room, and the bloody man snored so badly that I didn't get any sleep.

'After about four or five years of this I couldn't take it any longer and I would say going down in the car, "Right, Fred, we're not sharing the same room tonight. I need some

Fred Daly *(far right)* **pictured with Gene Sarazen** *(centre)* **and Bobby Locke at the 1976 Open Championship at Birkdale.**

Chapter 2

Harry Bradshaw

Harry Bradshaw hits a fairway wood during the Match Play Championships at Walton Heath (September 1955).

If story-telling could be measured in golfing terms, Harry Bradshaw would have played off scratch.

Up until his death in 1990, he was the father figure of Irish golf. A genial man, he had a common touch and people warmed to his easy-going manner. Great sportsmen are admired and often respected. 'The Brad', as he became known, was loved. For ten years after the Second World War he was Ireland's best golfer and when he stepped out on to the world stage he helped take Irish golf to a new level.

Harry Bradshaw pictured at the Silver King Tournament, Moor Park (April 1952).

As a member of Ireland's great triumvirate, Harry was the link between Fred Daly and Christy O'Connor. He partnered Daly to Ryder Cup success in 1953 and later helped O'Connor to Canada Cup glory in 1958.

The Ryder Cup was close to Bradshaw's heart, but he rated his Canada Cup success above all else. He may have lost a play-off for the individual prize, but it was still a personal triumph for Harry. A portly 45 year old, he coped with the heat and the altitude of Mexico City to put Irish golf on the world map.

'Bradshaw is my ideal golfer', wrote Henry Longhurst, the doyen of golf writers, 'successful but completely unspoiled; approachable on the course and affable and good-humoured off it, still managing to keep golf a game while making it his business. He can size up a shot, choose his club, hit the ball and be walking after it — all in the time it takes some to test the direction of the wind.'

● ● ● ●

Harry was born in 1913 in the village of Killincarrig, Co. Wicklow, about a mile from Delgany Golf Club. His father Ned was the professional at Delgany and within a few years the family moved to a house close to the course where Harry, the oldest of six siblings, quickly fell in love with the game.

It was clear in those early years that Harry had an aptitude for golf, and growing up on a course gave him ample opportunity to work on his game. He made the most of it and practised hard to develop a technique and approach to the game that worked for him.

It could never be said that he had a textbook swing. He had an unusual grip with three fingers of his right hand overlapping the left, and he used a rounded, three-quarter swing. Bernard Darwin, golf writer with *The Times*, described it as 'rugged and rustic', while Harry's biographer, golf journalist Dermot Gilleece, remarked that where golfing technique was concerned, 'Harry was at all times a pragmatist.'

Regardless of the method, it proved successful, and Harry probably had the benefit of knowing that in golf he had a certain amount of 'divine intervention' on his side.

'From an early age, I was always reasonably good at the game, though I could never have been considered long, even when I used the orthodox Vardon grip,' claimed Harry.

'Putting was my weak spot until I underwent a period of training from the toughest taskmaster any young professional could have had. Father Gleeson was a curate in Bray and when we met he would ask me how I played in such and such a match.

He had an unusual grip with three fingers of his right hand overlapping the left, and he used a rounded, three-quarter swing.

Like his great friend, Fred Daly, Harry started off in the game by caddying and later he moved seamlessly into the assistant's role at Delgany alongside his father.

'Almost invariably, I would have to report that I did very well except for my putting. "I'll have to take you in hand," he said. I would have been terrified out of

Harry Bradshaw plays over the ropes at the 15th during the Open Championship at Lytham St Annes (July 1952).

the game if I knew what he had in store for me. "Now," he would say as we went out to play at Delgany, "whenever you get the ball on the green, you must hole it in one stroke."'

Harry recalls that on some occasions it took almost four hours for him to play nine holes, with Father Gleeson

insisting that they couldn't move on to the next hole until Harry holed out. The curate would sit on his golf bag at the side of the green while Harry repeatedly putted from the same spot.

'The same procedure was carried out on numerous evenings when Father Gleeson had time to spare, until

I began to dread the sight of the man,' said Harry.

Gradually, Harry realised that the secret to getting around in a reasonable amount of time was to hit his approach

Harry stayed at Delgany until 1941 when he took up the post of professional at Kilcroney Golf and Country Club near Bray. By that stage he was competing regularly in professional tournaments and had singled himself out as one of Ireland's brightest talents, winning the Bromford-Adgey Cup in 1938.

> "Now, whenever you get the ball on the green, you must hole it in one stroke."

shots nearer the hole. As a consequence, he devoted himself to getting up and down from 100 yards and in the process developed a short game that was envied around the world.

The move to Kilcroney proved to be an auspicious one for him. He met his wife Elizabeth at the club and as the war years continued he got married, started a family and established himself as a prolific winner.

Harry Bradshaw *(back row, second from left)* **pictured with the GB & I Ryder Cup team including Fred Daly** *(front row, second from right)* **at Wentworth (1953).**

Harry dominated the Irish professional scene for the best part of 20 years (he won the Irish Professional Championship ten times) and in the process became a household name on these shores, a position that was cemented when he won the Irish Open at Royal Portrush in 1947 holding off, among others, Fred Daly.

Daly had won the Open Championship at Royal Liverpool and came to Portrush chasing a unique double. In the end he was some way off the pace as Harry's four rounds of 73, 74, 73 and 70 gave him victory by two shots over Belgian Flory van Donck.

Harry and Fred were rivals on the course but otherwise good friends and travelling companions. They had travelled to Royal Liverpool together and stayed in the same guest house throughout the Open.

Fred's victory in the Open was a breakthrough for Irish golfers. It was supposed to herald a wave of Irish success and Harry was seen as Fred's natural successor. He was next in line to win the biggest prize in golf and but for some outrageous misfortune, he might well have lifted the famous claret jug in 1949 at Royal St George's, Sandwich.

Harry travelled to Sandwich in great form and was encouraged when he led qualifying with rounds of 67 and 72 ahead of stars like Bobby Locke and Max Faulkner. He continued to play well in the opening round on Wednesday, finishing with a 68 which left him one off the pace.

Harry started his second round steadily until he came to the 5th, a long par four of 420 yards. He hit his tee shot and watched as the strong breeze pushed it towards the light rough.

He wasn't unduly concerned. But when he reached the ball, he was stunned to find it in a broken bottle. He didn't know what to do and neither did his playing partner. Could he drop it out? Would he incur a penalty?

Harry Bradshaw (*far left*) pictured with (*from left to right*) Fred Daly, Norman Sutton and Peter Alliss, wait to tee off at the International Golf Competition. In the second round, Harry and Belgian Flory Van Donck equalled the course record of 66 (June 1955).

Harry Bradshaw finds his ball inside a broken bottle in the rough at the 5th hole during the Open Championship at Royal St George's, Sandwich. Rather than wait for a ruling, Harry played on and took a double bogey at the hole. He went on to lose the play-off to Bobby Locke (July 1949).

For 15 minutes he waited in the vain hope that someone might provide him with an answer, but with no officials to be seen and in an era without walkie-talkies, he eventually made the decision to play the ball. Grabbing his nine-iron he stepped up to the ball, closed his eyes and, turning his head away, swung at the bottle. It smashed into pieces, while the ball travelled a mere 20 yards further.

Harry finished with a six but was rattled by the incident and eventually signed for a 77. To his great

and Irish Ryder Cup team. Harry was 40 years old when he joined Fred Daly at Wentworth on a team captained by Henry Cotton.

In the period since his near miss at Sandwich, Harry had moved in 1950 from Kilcroney to the professional's post at Portmarnock and had also broken his duck in Britain by winning the inaugural Dunbar Open in Scotland

> # Harry's status within the PGA as an 'overseas player' effectively ruled him out of the reckoning for a place on the Ryder Cup team.

credit he responded to the setback by putting together two final rounds of 68 and 70 to lead in the clubhouse with a total of 283.

Locke was his nearest challenger and the South African conjured up a brilliant birdie at the 17th and followed it up with a par on the 18th to set up a 36-hole play-off. Unfortunately, the play-off proved to be a real anticlimax. Harry's game had gone off the boil while Locke was in no mood to be generous. He put together two rounds of 67 and 68 to beat Harry by 12 shots. It was a disappointing end, made worse for Harry when he learned that he would not be considered for the Ryder Cup matches which would be played later that year at Ganton.

Harry's status within the PGA as an 'overseas player' effectively ruled him out of the reckoning for a place on the Ryder Cup team. It would take the PGA another four years to amend their rules allowing him to make his debut at Wentworth in 1953 as part of the first British

in 1952. While other players had to cope with their games disintegrating as they reached middle age, Harry seemed to be getting better and his greatest triumphs were still ahead of him.

Going into the 1953 matches, Cotton sought to develop a team ethic. The GB & I players roomed together, practised together and discussed tactics — it almost paid off.

In selecting his foursomes pairings for day one, he opted to put the two Irishmen together, a decision that suited both men. It was a natural pairing. Fred and Harry knew each other well and had played together regularly in challenge matches. Harry later asserted that he and Fred were never beaten in a match.

With Fred leading the way as the more experienced

Harry Bradshaw drives from the 10th during the Open Championship at Royal St George's, Sandwich (July 1949).

partner, the Irishmen started well against the American pairing of Walter Burkemo and Cary Middlecroft and finished the morning leading by three holes. The Americans fought back after lunch, but with nine holes remaining, Bradshaw and Daly had regained their three-hole advantage.

With the finish line in sight the Irishmen faltered and in the face of some inspired play from Burkemo,

the lead was trimmed to one with just the 18th left to play.

'Fred and I were coming up the 18th. I hit a bad drive into the left semi-rough and then Fred hit a wood right up to near the green,' said Harry.

'There were 25,000 people there — they were hanging out of the trees. I was left with a shot of 60, maybe 70 yards so I walked up to have a look. My two knees were knocking looking at this shot. I had never played in front of a crowd like it in my life.

'I came back and I said to Fred, "I don't know whether to play a nine or a ten," and he said, "Just play what you like." The mere fact that he did that gave me a lot of confidence — it doesn't matter what club you hit, so to speak. He didn't say like most people would have said, "Leave it close and I'll hole the putt."

'So I knocked it in to six feet and Fred holed it while they missed their chance for three. There was a mad rush for Fred and I often said to him, only the police were there, they'd have knocked him into the hole after the ball.'

The Irish win proved to be the only moment of joy on another disappointing day for GB & I. The team trailed 3-1 and Cotton threatened to 'kick their

Haas, who had been left out on day one by US captain Lloyd Mangrum.

Harry led by one at lunch and stretched that lead in the afternoon to record his second Ryder Cup victory by a 3 and 2 margin. Unfortunately, the Irish heroics weren't enough to ensure victory for GB & I. Rookies Peter Alliss and Bernard Hunt buckled under the pressure and the Americans retained the cup by a narrow one-point margin.

Two years later, Harry was part of the GB & I Ryder Cup team that travelled to play the Americans at the Thunderbird Ranch and Country Club in Palm Springs, California. For many of the GB & I team it was their first taste of desert-style golf and they all struggled in the unusual conditions, particularly getting used to the Bermuda grass which tended to grab and hold the ball.

The Americans fought back after lunch, but with nine holes remaining, Bradshaw and Daly had regained their three-hole advantage.

backsides'. Chastened by some hard words from their captain, GB & I came out with all guns blazing for the singles on day two, with the Irishmen again playing a starring role.

Dai Rees, off first, lost to Jack Burke, but behind him Fred Daly simply destroyed Ted Kroll 9 and 7. Further victories for Harry Weetman and Eric Brown suddenly left the teams level with four matches out on the course. Harry, full of confidence after his foursomes win, had been given the anchor role by Cotton. He faced Fred

Harry was now recognised as an integral member of the side. He had firmly established himself as one of the leading players on tour with victories in the 1953 and 1955 Dunlop Masters.

Captain Dai Rees was without the services of Fred Daly, but the former Open champion had been replaced by another Irishman, Christy O'Connor. While Christy was left out of the opening day foursomes, Harry and Rees faced the top American pairing of Sam Snead and Cary Middlecroft.

The Americans got off to a bright start and dominated the early holes, but gradually they were pegged back and by lunch the sides were level. Harry and Rees grabbed the first hole after lunch to take the lead, but despite recording ten 3's in the course of the match they still lost 3 and 2.

It proved to be another disappointing opening day for GB & I with John Fallon and John Jacobs recording the only win of the day. Rees summed up the problems facing his team: 'The plight of all British players today was putting. It is really something when Bradshaw does not make a putt.'

In the singles, Harry faced Jack Burke and after a poor opening nine holes, he fought back coming home in 31 to go into lunch all square. Harry was round in 65 but it was still only good enough to be level with Burke. The American responded after lunch, going out in 33 to engineer a three-hole lead which he maintained on his way to a 3 and 2 victory.

All in all, it proved to be an unsatisfactory trip for Harry. He had lost both his matches and once again GB & I had failed in their bid to regain the Ryder Cup. But that was set to change two years later at Lindrick.

By general consensus, the GB & I team assembled at Lindrick was one of the strongest for years, in stark contrast to the American side which was shorn of a number of star names. Sam Snead and Ben Hogan stayed at home, while Cary Middlecroft and Julius Boros were not selected after refusing to play in the PGA Championship.

Harry Bradshaw *(left)* and Christy O'Connor pictured with their caddies ahead of the Canada Cup World Golf Tournament in Tokyo (October 1957).

Harry Bradshaw plays from a bunker during the Professional Golfers' Match Play Championship at Walton Heath (September 1955).

Rees, back as GB & I captain, sought every advantage he could find. It was claimed that Lindrick, near Sheffield, was hand-picked by the competitive Welshman because he knew it so well. An inland course, it was relatively short, and Rees ensured it was set up to play hard and fast, almost like a links course.

Harry, returning for his third and final crack at the Americans, was 44 years old and had been out of the winner's enclosure since his Dunlop Masters victory in 1955. Christy O'Connor was also back, now a key member of the GB & I team which included only one rookie, Peter Mills.

Harry was left out of the foursomes on day one, during which GB & I made their usual poor start. The only victory of the day for the home side came from Rees, who partnered Ken Bousfield to victory over Art Wall and Fred Hawkins.

It certainly wasn't the start Rees had expected and he gathered his team together for a meeting to discuss selection for the singles. After some debate Max Faulkner and Harry Weetman were replaced by Bradshaw and Peter Mills. Weetman was disgusted by the decision and vowed he would never again play on a team captained by Rees.

It was an incident that could have done great damage to the team spirit, but the negative press generated by Weetman's comments only served to spur the team on to a famous victory.

Rees, showing great faith in his former partner, put Harry out last of the eight singles against the reigning US Open champion Dick Mayer.

'Christy came to me after the foursomes and said, "Who are you playing?" I said I'm playing Dick Mayer,' said Harry.

'"Oh," he says, putting his hands to his face, "Brad, I feel sorry for you. He's after beating myself and Eric

While Harry's battle with Mayer continued, the rest of the GB & I team were turning the tables on their American opponents, inflicting a series of heavy defeats. With Harry still out on the course, Ken Bousfield closed out Lionel Herbert 4 and 3 to win the Ryder Cup.

With the cheers from the crowd ringing around them, Harry and Mayer sought gamely to finish their match. After slipping behind again, Harry won the 14th to level things, and the two men halved the remaining holes to finish on the 18th all square in front of massive crowds.

Observer journalist Pat Ward Thomas described the scene. 'Suddenly, before anyone could believe it, the

> ## 'We were drinking champagne until 5 o'clock in the morning,' he said. 'They went mad that day.'

Brown 7 and 6." I said, I'll knock in putt for putt with him.'

Harry was as good as his word and, following the promising start made by his team mates, he won the first three holes, including holing a bunker shot at the 3rd.

Harry continued: 'Walking to the 4th tee Mayer said to me, "You're a great trap player, Harry." Yes, I said, I hole four or five in a round as a rule. He said, "I hope you don't do that this morning." I was giving him the old one and two.'

After his bright start, Harry let Mayer back into the match and at lunch the American held a one-hole lead. Harry levelled things by winning the opening hole of the second 18, and from then on there was never more than a hole in it.

deed was done, the Americans had been put to flight as never before. . . . Last of all Bradshaw brought a wonderful even match with Mayer to its fitting end by getting down in two from well short of the last green. An unforgettable day was done.'

Harry felt he should really have come away with a full point. He three-putted the 9th green twice and blamed it for his failure to finish his Ryder Cup career with another win. He was, however, part of a remarkable victory, one that did wonders for golfing morale across the British Isles, and he certainly enjoyed the celebrations that followed.

'We were drinking champagne until 5 o'clock in the morning,' he said. 'They went mad that day.'

Chapter 3

Christy O'Connor

Christy O'Connor in action.

Harry Bradshaw knew a good thing when he saw it.

In 1954 'The Brad' beat a Bundoran-based professional in a 36-hole play-off for the Irish Professional Championship at Royal County Down.

'I'm afraid I'm on the way out,' he said afterwards. 'This young man, Christy O'Connor, is the player to watch out for in the future.'

Three years later, Harry and Christy were members of the GB & I side that engineered a famous Ryder Cup victory at Lindrick. Christy's outstanding singles performance in a bitterly contested match with Dow Finsterwald confirmed to many what Harry had known for a long time. The Galway man was blessed with sublime ability, but he also had a fierce competitive streak and a ruthlessness which came to the fore at Lindrick.

Christy O'Connor drives off at the 2nd at Royal Birkdale during practice ahead of the Ryder Cup (October 1965).

In his autobiography written by John Redmond, Christy described the match with Finsterwald as 'a classic — with needle'.

The antagonism between the two men arose from an incident that occurred on the 3rd green. Christy started the match brightly and won the opening two holes with birdies to grab a two-hole lead. He found the 3rd green with his approach, while his opponent missed the green and chipped up to around six feet. Christy putted first and rolled his ball two feet past the hole. Finsterwald needed to hole his for par, but when the ball slid by the hole he reached out and hooked it back with his putter.

'The crowd encircling the green gasped in astonishment and before I had time to do or say a thing, the referee moved on to the green and announced, "O'Connor three

up,"' stated Christy. Finsterwald protested that he had not conceded the hole, but the referee stood his ground and Christy suddenly had a three-hole advantage.

Harry Bradshaw was playing Dick Mayer in the last match of the day immediately behind Christy and Finsterwald. He was watching the American as he walked to the 4th tee and saw him cracking his driver off the ground.

'I said to myself, something must have happened,' recalled Harry. 'I wasn't too long finding out. Every Irish doctor in England seemed to be following Christy and myself and some Irish doctors told me what had happened walking to the 4th tee.' Harry later added that during lunch he sought Christy out and warned him to knock in every putt, even if it was only two or three inches from the hole.

Christy had other things on his mind as he sat down to a quick bowl of soup. A series of putting errors had allowed Finsterwald back into the match and they had finished the morning round all square. Christy simply

Christy was shocked to lose the hole. But if Finsterwald had hoped to knock Christy off his stride, he obviously didn't have the measure of his man. Incensed by what he saw as blatant gamesmanship, Christy proceeded to

Christy holed a string of putts to open up a six-hole lead after just eight holes of the afternoon round.

didn't feel comfortable on the greens, so during the break he took a gamble and switched to a lighter putter which he purchased from the pro shop at Lindrick.

The new club definitely seemed to have the desired effect. Christy holed a string of putts to open up a six-hole lead after just eight holes of the afternoon round. The atmosphere between the two men had been poisonous following the morning incident and Christy's blistering start to the afternoon did little to improve matters.

On the 9th green both men had short putts for par. Finsterwald putted first and missed. Christy conceded the return putt and Finsterwald strode off the green towards the 10th hole.

'When I putted, I just missed and since my ball came to rest no more than an inch from the hole, I assumed he would give it to me for the half and I picked it up,' stated Christy.

'I duly stepped forward with the honour to drive off the next tee, but as I prepared to hit my drive, Finsterwald broke the long silence between us. "Hold it," he shouted, "you did not finish out. I'm claiming the hole and it's my honour."'

Christy O'Connor shakes hands with America's Frank Beard after winning his singles match 5 and 4 at Royal Birkdale (September 1969).

Christy O'Connor (*back row, second from left*) **pictured with the 1965 GB & I Ryder Cup team including Jimmy Martin** (*front row, extreme right*) **at Royal Birkdale.**

win the 10th to regain his six-hole lead, stretched it to seven by winning the 11th and then sealed an emphatic 7 and 6 victory with a par on the 12th.

'He's the only golfer to my mind who could do that,' said Bradshaw. 'A good many golfers would have fallen apart after that happened — knowing that the hole was halved and then losing it by this little incident.'

It is perhaps not surprising that Christy coped so well with Finsterwald's antics at Lindrick. He came from the school of hard knocks and he took a teak-tough persona with him on to the course.

'They called me a big, moody boor who would not pass the time of day on the golf course,' he stated. 'Perhaps I was, but I did not mean to look so grim. It was my way of concentrating. Deep down I was happy at my work.'

Christy O'Connor loved the game. He still does, but it was a job.

Playing golf was about being the best you could be, pitting yourself against the best and, most importantly, making a living for your family. He once stated that he wasn't too sure if golf was a profession or a trade. Either way, hard work took Christy O'Connor to the top.

• • • •

There was a period when Christy O'Connor was Ireland's most famous sportsman. If he wasn't making some last day charge in search of a record cheque, he was out and about with some of his celebrity pals.

He was, in many respects, the first Irish sportsman to register on the world stage. His graceful swing

He harboured ambitions to try his hand on the tournament scene, but the Ryder Cup, which he would become synonymous with, never entered his mind.

'I wanted to be a player. In those early days I learnt a lot from Bob Wallace,' he said. 'I loved playing and I worked very hard to be a good player. You don't get it just by thinking about it.'

Christy's talent was obvious to the members at Galway and later at Tuam where he moved in 1948 as greenkeeper cum professional. There was a general consensus that here was a player who could compete with the best. Unfortunately, he met a wall of official resistance from the Irish Professional Golfers Association. It took him five years to be accepted as a member of the association and become eligible to play in official events — five years during which he built up

'I loved playing and I worked very hard to be a good player. You don't get it just by thinking about it.'

(honed through long hours of practice on the sands at Bundoran), his longevity (he won his last Irish Championship at the age of 51) and his ten consecutive Ryder Cup appearances kept him in the public eye.

It was a long way from the Galway farm he grew up on. Christy's father could never understand his son's fascination with a game he insisted 'was going to get him nowhere'. The family home bordered the first green at Galway Golf Club; like Fred Daly and Harry Bradshaw before him, Christy was soon consumed by golf.

He turned to caddying to make a few extra pennies and later took up the assistant's role under then club professional Bob Wallace. Those were contented times for Christy. He was 23 years old, working in a job he loved and playing golf at every opportunity.

a well of resentment and frustration at the injustice of a system that prevented him from competing against his peers.

When Christy finally did get his chance to play, it was with a sense of purpose, of steely determination that marked him out as different from everyone else. He was making up for lost time and lost earnings. It was serious business and he treated it as such.

Following a 19th place finish in the 1951 British Open in Royal Portrush, Christy took up the professional's post at Bundoran Golf Club in Donegal. It was the perfect move at that stage in his career as it gave him a base to become involved in regular tournament golf. The Northern branch of the IPGA had a busy fixture list and he grabbed every opportunity to compete.

The move to Bundoran was also significant in other ways. It was there that he met his future wife Mary Collins. Married in October 1954, they honeymooned at the Gleneagles Hotel in Scotland, where Christy won his first tournament outside Ireland.

In 1958 Christy moved from Bundoran to Killarney and that was quickly followed by another move in April 1959 to Royal Dublin.

'The general feeling among the players travelling to America was that we were on our way to be slaughtered, but in the circumstances let's do the best we can,' he said.

'And that was the feeling for many years. I am not totally condemning the captains of the time, but I believe they should have been more strong willed and in control of the team. They should have been telling

Christy made his breakthrough on the Irish scene in 1953 by winning the Ulster Championship and the Irish Dunlop crown.

'Tactically, it was the best decision I ever made,' he said. The championship links course allowed him to play golf all year round, and critically, with his growing travel commitments he also had an international airport on his doorstep.

Christy made his breakthrough on the Irish scene in 1953 by winning the Ulster Championship and the Irish Dunlop crown and then in 1955 he announced himself to the wider golfing community by winning the first four-figure cheque in European golf at the Swallow-Penfold tournament.

He also bagged his second Irish Dunlop crown in 1955 and a top-ten finish in the Open Championship at St Andrews secured his place on the Ryder Cup team scheduled to take place at the Thunderbird Ranch and Country Club in Palm Springs, California.

It turned out to be something of a mixed experience for Christy. He relished the opportunity to play in America for the first time, but he was immediately struck by the defeatist approach of the GB & I team. It was an attitude that he encountered on a regular basis throughout his years competing in the event.

our players, "let's go out and win", rather than what became the catch phrase, "let's go out and put up a good show."'

At least Christy had the support and advice of regular travelling companion Harry Bradshaw to rely on. The two men played well together in practice. It looked like an ideal pairing, but captain Dai Rees felt differently and left Christy out altogether on the day one foursomes.

The Galway man got his chance on day two as lead-off man in the singles against the legendary club thrower, Tommy 'Thunder' Bolt. As a Ryder Cup baptism, it probably went a long way to helping Christy cope with the antics of Finsterwald at Lindrick as he found himself not only having to deal with Bolt's notorious bad temper but also a caddie who appeared hell-bent on ensuring a win for America.

'It was my first visit to the United States and I tended to rely more on my caddie's club selection rather than my own instincts,' said Christy. The two men had worked well in practice and Christy was confident of performing well against Bolt.

He fell behind early in the 36-hole match, but at the 6th hole he looked in good shape to grab one back with his opponent stuck in a bunker. Standing in the middle of the fairway, Christy was handed a three-iron by his caddie and made a perfect

connection. Expecting to see the ball land on the putting surface, he was stunned as he watched it fly the green and land in a bush.

'I had been fooled. I was badly mis-clubbed and now I had lost a hole I should have won,' he said. 'As we progressed, the clubbing got worse and when we arrived at the 18th green I was three down.'

Christy was forced to take matters into his own hands, and as he headed for lunch he made it perfectly clear to

Christy O'Connor drives during the Ryder Cup at Lindrick (October 1957).

his caddie that he was not to offer him any more advice on club selection. Relying on his own instincts, he made an excellent start to the second 18 and quickly cut the deficit to one hole. Suddenly put under pressure, Bolt made a few mistakes and, reverting to type, started tossing clubs. Christy had him on the run, but then help arrived for the American in the shape of band

leader Phil Harris, an old friend of Bolt. Harris had a calming effect on him as he regained his composure and put his clubs to better use by closing out the match 4 and 2.

It was the first of many Ryder Cup defeats that Christy endured during his record-breaking run of

Christy O'Connor (*back row, extreme left*) pictured with the 1969 GB & I team at Royal Birkdale.

appearances. He freely admits that his own record is not particularly outstanding but, without making excuses, points to a couple of reasons which contributed to his modest tally of 13 points from 36 matches.

'Things have changed so much since I played in the Ryder Cup. When we took on the Americans we were still club professionals while they were full-time tournament players,' he said.

Many of Christy's best Ryder Cup performances came alongside renowned television commentator Peter Alliss. The two were first paired together at the Eldorado Country Club, Palm Springs, in the 1959 Ryder Cup. Facing Art Wall and Doug Ford, they combined well to record a 3 and 2 win, the only foursomes victory of the day for the visiting team.

Mind you, they were lucky to be playing at all, having been involved in a terrifying

The plane encountered a violent storm and plummeted 4,000 feet before the pilot managed to regain control.

'We were still teaching, trying to make a few bucks to support our families. It was difficult and it was very hard work. When I was in Bundoran I used to give lessons in the summer from 8.30 in the morning until dark, and then I went back to the shop and spent another couple of hours fixing clubs.'

As one of Europe's leading lights, Christy also played more often than some of his team mates and was regularly pitched against America's top players.

'Every team had passengers,' recalled Christy in Seamus Smith's tribute book, *Himself.* 'There were those who got sick, scared to death of the big occasions, and that added extra pressure on the top four or five players who had to play every match — and win!'

plane flight from Los Angeles to Palm Springs. Flying over the San Jacinto mountain range, the plane encountered a violent storm and plummeted 4,000 feet before the pilot managed to regain control and returned to Los Angeles.

Christy described the flight as the most terrifying experience of his life and recalled that, once back on the ground, everyone headed straight to a bar where brandy was consumed by the bottle.

The team, which included Belfast-based Norman Drew, later founded the 'Long Drop club' as a way of marking their brush with death. Club members must raise a glass and toast each of the co-founders at 5.30 p.m. on 29 October every year.

Christy O'Connor plays from a bunker on the Old Course at St Andrews during the Alcan Golfer of the Year tournament (October 1967).

The frightening experience brought the team together but it didn't have any effect on the outcome. GB & I lost the Ryder Cup by a heavy margin. However, the O'Connor/Alliss partnership survived that defeat and thrived in future Ryder Cup battles. Between 1959 and 69 they played 12 matches together, winning five, losing six and halving one.

'I spent a lot of time playing with Christy and he was a wonderful partner to have,' said Alliss.

'We got on very well together on the golf course. He was brave, he just had a wonderful aura about him. I remember on one of the early holes (in 1959) I hit the ball into the bushes and apologised to Christy. He

turned and asked me if I was doing my best, and when I told him that I was, he said, "Well then, never apologise to me again." And I never did.'

In many ways it was an unusual pairing. The two men were not particularly friendly and came from completely different backgrounds, but together they made a formidable pairing on the course.

'I always did my best for Christy and, God knows, he did his best for me. I had the most amazing confidence in him,' added Peter.

'Neither of us was a good putter, yet we holed putts when it mattered. We became a very solid partnership. I especially remember Royal Birkdale in 1965, where Christy and I won two games out of four.

Christy O'Connor chats with Tom Haliburton on the putting green at Wentworth ahead of the second day of play in the Daks Tournament (June 1960).

Christy O'Connor holds aloft the trophy after winning the Irish Hospitals Trust event at Woodbrook, Co. Wicklow (July 1960).

'We played some wonderful golf in the foursomes on the opening afternoon, beating Billy Casper and Gene Littler. But the following morning we got a terrible hammering from Arnold Palmer and Dave Marr. That was a very unusual occurrence for us and, by way of proving it, we went on to beat the same pair on the 18th in the afternoon. I tell you, over the years O'Connor and I had the ability to surprise the best that America could throw at us.'

morning and afternoon singles on the final day.

'I reckon I did as much as I could to vindicate his confidence in me,' said Christy later. Playing J. C. Snead in the morning, Christy shot 71, the best round by the home side, but he still lost by one hole. In the afternoon, facing US Open champion Tom Weiskopf, he was one down with four to play, but won the 15th to level matters and then got up and down from a greenside

> 'We played some wonderful golf in the foursomes on the opening afternoon, beating Billy Casper and Gene Littler.'

The pair played together for the last time in 1969 at Royal Birkdale, halving a foursomes match with Billy Casper and Frank Beard. Christy, at 45 years of age, was still a leading light in the GB & I team and won three of his four matches at Birkdale.

The 1969 Ryder Cup saw the first tie between the sides, with Jack Nicklaus conceding Tony Jacklin's two-foot putt on the 18th green. It was a memorable occasion for everyone involved although, put in the same position, Christy doubted whether he would have been as generous as Nicklaus.

Four years later, Christy bowed out of the Ryder Cup at Muirfield. He was 49 years old but still capable of superb golf, as emphasised by a remarkable round of 61 during practice. He covered the back nine in 29 shots that day and remarked afterwards that it was the right score on the wrong day!

Captain Bernard Hunt clearly had no worries about Christy's age affecting his performance. He played five matches in total (partnering Neil Coles on three occasions) and returned one and half points for his captain. Hunt's faith in Christy was such that with the event finely balanced after two days at 8-8, he played him in both the

bunker to halve the match. It was a typically gutsy performance from Christy and a fitting end to his Ryder Cup career.

'They were great times and I have some magnificent memories,' said Christy. His one regret, though, is that he was never asked to captain the side.

'I would have loved it. With my experience I might have been able to do the job better than others, maybe, but only with full control,' he said.

Chapter 4

Norman Drew

Norman Drew plays a shot watched by Keith MacDonald at the Martini Golf Tournament at the Berkshire Club (August 1960).

Doug Ford wasn't worried but he was angry with himself as he stood on the 35th tee all square.

He knew he had let his opponent back into the match, not once, but twice. A less experienced man could have been shaken, but he was Doug Ford, 1957 Masters winner playing in his third Ryder Cup, and he had worked out what was wrong.

He took his driver from his bag and giving it a few waggles turned to his opponent. 'I'm going to slow my swing down and beat you,' he said.

Norman Drew looked back at Ford. 'If that's the case,' replied the 27-year-old assistant professional from Knock Golf Club in Belfast, 'you'd better knock a couple in then.'

It was perhaps inevitable that a boy who grew up in the shadow of Fred Daly would one day emulate him by playing in the Ryder Cup.

Growing up on the fairways of Belfast's Balmoral Golf Club, Norman Drew didn't just listen to tales of the great man's deeds, he lived them. The former British Open champion regularly threw the youngster out of his shop with orders to 'get away and practise'.

'As a boy you were aware that Fred had won the Open and Fred was playing in this, going to that and had been selected for the Ryder Cup,' said Norman.

'He was the king at that time, match play champion, British Open champion and a real super guy. If it

hadn't been for the war, who knows what he might have done.'

Daly may have lost the best of his competitive years to the war, but his triumphs opened the eyes of a generation of young Irish golfers and set Norman on course for his own date with the Ryder Cup and his singles clash with Doug Ford.

Norman was playing the best golf of his career when he secured his berth in the GB & I team for the 1959 matches at the Eldorado Country Club in Palm Springs. Victory in the Yorkshire Evening News event put him into contention, and he followed that up by winning the Irish PGA in August 1959 before finishing second in the Irish Masters at Portmarnock.

Norman Drew (*front row, second from right*) **pictured with the GB & I Ryder Cup team including Christy O'Connor** (*back row, far right*) **at Palm Desert, California (1959).**

'After winning the Yorkshire I realised that I was in a position to qualify for the Ryder Cup. I knew that if I played steady for the rest of the season, I would finish high enough up the order of merit to make the team,' said Norman.

In fact, a strong showing in the July Irish Hospitals tournament helped him to finish sixth in the order of merit with a points total of 337.9.

In making the team, he created his own bit of history by becoming the first Irishman to play in both the Walker Cup and the Ryder Cup. Unusual at the time, it's a path well worn today by, among others, Ronan Rafferty and Padraig Harrington.

The Walker Cup pits the best amateurs of GB & I against the best in America in a biennial match play format. Norman made his only Walker Cup appearance in 1953 at the Kittansett Club in Marian, Massachusetts. It was the culmination of a glittering amateur career which saw him win Irish caps in 1952 and 53 on the back of victories in the East of Ireland and the North of Ireland championships.

It would be wrong to assume that the teenage Norman dreamt about playing in the Ryder Cup. The event did not have the prestige and the kudos it has today. As a

the Ryder Cup team came as a result of his excellent tournament play and not as part of any 'grand plan' to qualify.

In 1959, Norman had been married to his wife Valerie for just over a year and he was working as an assistant professional at Knock Golf Club in Belfast. He had been a professional for five years, starting out with Sam Bacon in County Armagh Golf Club before moving to the north-west for a spell and then returning to Belfast.

'I thought I was well paid as a full-time pro. I used to get £5 a week as a full professional, £2.50 as an assistant,' said Norman.

'I actually played in the Ryder Cup as an assistant. Let me tell you, very few assistant professionals played in the Ryder Cup.'

The move back to Belfast was calculated to help Norman's chances in tournament play, and the assistant role gave him the freedom he needed to compete more regularly on the fledgling professional circuit. Settled in Belfast with his wife and a regular income from his job at Knock, he made the most of the opportunity and had his best year on tour, culminating in his appearance at the Eldorado Country Club.

'After winning the Yorkshire I realised that I was in a position to qualify for the Ryder Cup.'

gifted amateur, his one ambition had been to play for Ireland, which he did to great effect. His record in the Home Internationals for the years 1952 and 53 reads: played 12, won eight, drew two and lost two.

His Walker Cup selection was in recognition of that superb consistency and, similarly, his inclusion in

Today we think of selection for the Ryder Cup as being the pinnacle of a professional golfer's career. There is great honour attached, but also a huge degree of pressure and in some cases downright terror.

In 1959, Norman was singularly unphased about the prospect of squaring up to the best America could

> ## 'I was made to feel welcome right away. I was just another player to them.'

muster. He didn't seek out Fred Daly for any advice; he didn't even discuss it to any great extent with his peers.

'The only time I spoke about it at all was when the team assembled at Gleneagles for some fitness checks and to select the final three players for the team,' he said.

'I wasn't nervous about it. I had played amateur golf to the highest level and I had been a professional for five years. I had some idea of what I could do and what to expect in the professional arena.'

Norman knew he was playing well and, more importantly, he also knew he could call on an amateur background which put a premium on match play expertise.

'As an amateur it was all match play, but as a pro it was all stroke play apart from the News of the World event which I didn't enter very often,' said Norman.

'But it wasn't something new to me. I had lots of match play experience and I knew that in match play, chipping and putting were very important and I was strong in both those areas. My choice of golf now is stroke play. That's the true result of a game, but back then I knew what to do in a match play situation.'

● ● ● ●

Standing on the 17th tee at Eldorado, Norman was having to call on all his match play expertise.

'The final two holes were both par fours, but the 17th had proved easy during the practice rounds. It was a dog-leg and players had been smashing the ball over the corner and getting on in two,' said Norman.

'But overnight they imported a big tree and planted it in the corner. Well, Ford lined up at that palm tree and hit a huge drive right over the top of it. He then fired in a second shot which finished up eight feet from the hole.

'I had been forced to play around the tree, which meant the green was definitely out of reach. I still managed my par, but he slotted his putt home for a birdie. It meant that I was one down with one to play.'

● ● ● ●

The seven men who gathered in Gleneagles in late September found themselves in an unusual position — they were the holders of the trophy.

The 1957 team, captained by Welshman Dai Rees and including Irish heroes Harry Bradshaw and Christy O'Connor, had stunned the golfing world by beating the Americans at Lindrick.

'I was made to feel welcome right away. I was just another player to them, capable of playing good golf. They were well aware of my play during the two years following the Lindrick result and understood that my position on the order of merit was justified,' said Norman.

Rees, installed again as captain for the 1959 event, claimed: 'We are the trophy holders and we will start off just that bit more confidently than before. The boot will be on the other foot for the Americans.'

Norman Drew (*back row, extreme left*) **and Christy O'Connor** (*back row, third from left*) **with members of the GB & I Ryder Cup team on their arrival in New York aboard the liner** *Queen Elizabeth* **(October 1959).**

He had every right to feel confident. Apart from Drew and Dave Thomas who were cup rookies, eight of the side that triumphed in Lindrick were back for the trip to America.

However, not everything went smoothly in Gleneagles. The selection process for the final three places caused some consternation among the players assembled.

Each player was asked to nominate the men to fill the last three berths and when the votes were counted, Ken Bousfield, Eric Brown and Dave Thomas were selected. Brown was the most contentious selection. The Scot had struggled with a back injury for most of the season and had been unable to play in the qualifying events.

He had, however, been Great Britain's best performer during the Lindrick victory and towards the end of August he reappeared on tour declaring himself fit again. He played in a foursomes event in Sherwood Forest and then the News of the World Match Play in September, but despite playing well he failed on both occasions to find the winner's circle.

'A few of us were stunned by the outcome. I voted for Hitchcock and Lester, the next two men on the order of merit, as did Peter Mills and O'Connor. We couldn't understand how it (selection) happened,' said Norman.

The team quickly put the incident behind them and boarded the *Queen Elizabeth* liner on 14 October for the trip to America. Rees, speaking to the press ahead of their departure, stated that the boat journey would provide four days of 'complete rest and relaxation'.

'It will give the players a rest and also allow them to acclimatise more slowly,' he added.

He couldn't have been more wrong. The boat journey was the first sign of the travel problems which dogged the team and later almost cost them their lives.

'Right from the start, the team made a mistake by travelling by boat. As soon as we got out to sea the weather turned bad. It was rough. They had to close the pools, there were no deck games, no table-tennis, nothing to do,' added Norman.

'They had a net on board to practise in, but you simply couldn't stand up. The team used to go for a wander around the deck, but the numbers declined daily as seasickness took hold. It was a great relief when we finally arrived in America.'

Once in America, the team spent a week in Atlantic City getting organised and practising together before setting off across the US.

It's important to understand that these golfers were not the highly paid professionals of today. This was a working trip and the team played in a number of Pro-Ams and events as they travelled across the country to Palm Springs.

'We were all professionals who played for a living and the matches were a way of making some money which was split 11 ways,' added Norman. It also served as vital practice for the team and gave Rees the opportunity to consider his pairings for the matches.

Norman Drew *(far right)* **pictured with** *(from left)* **M. Ferguson (Austria), Gary Player (South Africa), Max Faulkner (England), Dick Metz (USA) at the Irish Hospitals Trust competition (July 1960).**

Before any of that, however, the team had to get to Palm Springs and they almost didn't make it.

'We were flying from Washington to LA. Four or five of us were sitting in the back playing whist for a few dollars when the pilot told us all that we were coming into bad weather and instructed the passengers to get into their seats and put their seat-belts on,' said Norman.

'It was around four o'clock in the afternoon and it got very dark, so dark that the lights had to go on in the plane. The pilot told us that if he got a chance to land he would, but if he couldn't put the plane down he would have to go somewhere else.

'So we're all strapped in and the plane starts to descend and then, bang, out of the clouds we touch down no problem. We grabbed our gear and we were told there was a charter flight waiting to take us from LA to Palm Springs.

'All the service flights had been cancelled by the storm, but as a charter flight all the pilot needed was a clear runway and he made the decision to take us back into the storm.

The pilot somehow managed to fly the plane between two peaks of the San Jacinto mountain range. However, the plane was then forced to return to LA because the storm had closed the Palm Springs airport.

'When we got back to LA someone had to contact Palm Springs to tell everyone we were all right,' added Norman.

'That flight should have taken three-quarters of an hour, but we finished up making another bad decision and opted to go on to Palm Springs by coach. That was nearly as bad because we then spent two and half hours driving on narrow mountain roads!'

It was a terrifying experience for the whole team, and although the players founded the Long Drop club in memory of their survival, it clearly had a bad effect on the team.

'It did a lot of damage to everyone's nerves. You get these flash thoughts — I could have been in a box instead of playing golf,' said Norman.

In Norman's view, poor travel plans played a large part in the team's failure to retain the trophy.

> ## It's important to understand that these golfers were not the highly paid professionals of today.

'I remember sitting in that plane reading a magazine, when it just flew out of my hands and hit the ceiling before floating down slowly. We were later told we had dropped 4,000 feet.'

According to Norman, people in Palm Springs were waiting for Bob Hutcheon, the Pennsylvanian steel baron who had sponsored the GB & I trip to America, and saw the plane simply disappear from view.

'I played on two teams (Walker Cup and Ryder Cup) that travelled to America, and on both occasions the actual travelling did a lot of damage. There was too much of it and it took too long,' he said.

Finally settled in Palm Springs, the GB & I side tried to focus on the task ahead. The days preceding the matches took on a familiar pattern for the players as Rees juggled his pairings in between practice sessions.

Norman Drew in action at the Gor-Ray Cup Assistants Golf Championships (June 1955).

Norman had been confident of playing both days. His form prior to the Ryder Cup week had been very good, but his touch deserted him in Palm Springs and by his own admission he didn't play well.

'I certainly didn't play as well as I could have played or even as well as I'd played in Atlantic City. During our time there I'd been paired with O'Connor, Weetman, Thomas and Mills. We played a bit of a sweep every day and I think my pairing won three times,' said Norman.

'I think by the time the matches came around I was tired, not physically, but mentally. The heat played a

'I wasn't worried about it at all. The American team was full of first-class operators but they were golfers just like me,' said Norman.

'You can't play on a team feeling you shouldn't be there. I was as good as anyone in Britain at that time, and I really didn't care who I played against. He was going to have to play well.'

As a rookie, Norman could have done with the support of a close-knit unit, but there seems to have been little effort to bring the players together as a team. He can't remember going to the type of team meetings we think

> **'You can't play on a team feeling you shouldn't be there.
> I was as good as anyone in Britain at that time.'**

part and so did the travelling. I had just played too much.'

The Eldorado course was relatively new and speaking to the press, Christy O'Connor and Norman both felt the cup would be won on the greens. In Norman's opinion, the course wasn't too hard and certainly not overly long. Orange groves and palm trees were the major hazards and there was precious little rough.

It was set up for a straight hitter who was good around the greens, ideal conditions for the assistant from Knock. Unfortunately, his game had gone off the boil. Possibly, although he doesn't admit it, maybe Norman finally realised he was playing in the Ryder Cup.

The American team was packed with stars of the era, Sam Snead, Cary Middlecroft and, of course, Doug Ford. The crowds, mostly American, built up through the week and the anticipation grew with each day. However, Norman insists there was no sense of awe, no inferiority complex.

of as integral to Ryder Cup matches today. He gravitated towards his friend and part-time travelling companion, Peter Mills, and he naturally spent time with the other Irishman in the team, Christy O'Connor.

It is clear that Rees was very much in control and, according to Norman, he simply announced the pairings over breakfast or dinner.

'He probably had more power than any of us realised at the time,' said Norman.

'He never said that much to me. In fact, the only conversation we had was when he took me aside after the foursomes and told me to get to bed early because I was out first in the singles.

'In general, I got on well with the man. When we played on tour, he would sometimes invite me to have dinner with him. He always stayed in first-class hotels, which of course the rest of us didn't. But I would go round and we would have some dinner and a chat.'

Norman was disappointed to be dropped for the foursomes but, along with Mills who had injured his back and failed to play any part in the event, he took on the role of team man and spent the day on a buggy travelling between matches. If nothing else, it helped him soak up the atmosphere, and when Rees pulled him aside to tell him he was out first the next day, he was ready to go.

The perceived wisdom has always been that Norman was a 'sacrificial lamb' in the singles matches. Guessing that Sam Snead would put one of his big guns out first, Rees decided to sacrifice one of his 'lesser lights' in the hope of maybe matching one of his 'more accomplished' players with a weaker American opponent.

playing in the singles, shaking his head at me. So I went for it with my three-wood. It was the best fairway wood I ever hit and it stopped around 15 feet from the hole.'

It was a superb strike under pressure, and although Ford responded by firing an iron into the green close to the pin, Norman dropped his putt to halve the match.

Norman continued: 'I shook his hand and said, "I enjoyed the game but I don't think you did." I headed into the locker room and I saw two men sitting there having a drink. One was Tarzan (Johnny Weizmuller) and the other was Bing Crosby's brother, Bob. They asked me if I was the guy who had just holed out on the 18th and then invited me to have a drink with them.'

> # 'I shook his hand and said, "I enjoyed the game but I don't think you did."'

It's an idea hotly disputed today by Norman, and standing on the 36th tee at Eldorado, one down to Ford, he had no doubt that he was the right man in the right place.

'The 18th at Eldorado had water down the left and water crossing the fairway in two places,' continued Norman.

'Ford hit off first but played a bit safe, going left and ending any chance he had of reaching the green in two. My caddie said to me, you had better take a new ball and hit it over that water hazard, which was around 225 yards from the tee. That was right on the limit for me, but I hit it well and found the fairway.

'Ford had to lay up short of the second hazard that crossed the fairway close to the green, and I was tempted to do the same. I was reaching for an iron when I saw my team mate Peter Mills, who was not

Norman's three-wood approach is recognised as one of the great moments of the Ryder Cup and was all the more remarkable coming from a player who was considered a shortish hitter.

'I have always disagreed with the sacrificial lamb notion,' added Norman.

'We were a point down going into the singles matches. You wouldn't put a rubbish player out first. You don't want to go two down straight away. You would want to make sure that at the very least you got a half. At the time, the decision to put me out first made perfect sense.'

● ● ● ●

GB & I went into the singles matches of the 1959 Ryder Cup trailing by just a point, but they found themselves

Norman Drew

Norman Drew pictured in Malone Golf Club, Belfast (July 1978).

swamped on the final day. Norman and Peter Alliss were the only players to pick up any points, and the team lost 8½-3½. Speaking afterwards, Rees declared that 'Drew and Alliss would spearhead the 1961 Ryder Cup team.'

The Welshman was half-right. While Alliss went on to play in five further cups, Norman never again reached the heights of his play in 1959.

'It never really bothered me that I didn't play in the Ryder Cup again and I don't know why. I don't like to dwell on decisions I made in the past. I went to South Africa to play and it probably wasn't the right move. I wasn't able to pick up any order of merit points down there.

'But I thoroughly enjoyed playing in the cup. It suited me. I was a competitive golfer; I always had to play for something. I still do, even if it's just a pound.'

> 'It was quite strange. There weren't the crowds like there are now. It was just us, the team, and we were all very disappointed.'

There was little or no interest in the Ryder Cup when the players returned to Great Britain, especially after such a heavy defeat. There was even less interest in Belfast. Many people didn't know and didn't really care that Norman had hit one of the great Ryder Cup shots.

Norman just got on with his job, which was following the money of professional golf. He decided to play on the South African Tour in 1960 and somewhere along the way he lost his swing and ultimately his game.

He took his young family and moved to Scotland where he became a club pro at a club called Ralston, near Paisley. He later returned to Northern Ireland where he worked as a club pro up until his retirement. He had family responsibilities and he simply couldn't afford to go chasing after tournament money.

'It was very disappointing to lose the cup,' said Norman.

'It was quite strange. There weren't the crowds like there are now. It was just us, the team, and we were all very disappointed.

Chapter 5

Jimmy Martin

Jimmy Martin drives from the 2nd tee during the Swallow-Penfold Tournament (May 1961).

The Ryder Cup is not to everyone's taste. There is too much pressure, too much expectation and far too much media attention for some golfers to cope with.

Take Jimmy Martin, for instance. One of Ireland's top touring pros in the 1960s, Jimmy played in the 1965 Ryder Cup at Royal Birkdale and was singularly underwhelmed by the entire experience.

Close friend and regular travelling companion, Nicky Lynch, claims that Jimmy refused to wear his Ryder Cup blazer in the years following the event.

'He also had a lovely Ryder Cup bag which he never used either,' said Nicky, who is the resident professional at Sutton Golf Club, a position he has held for 50 years.

'I used to go on at him to use the bag and wear the blazer, but he'd say, "Why would I want to do that? Sure everyone would know who you are then." He preferred to use an old battered brown bag that he had for years. But that was Jimmy — he just wanted to go quietly about his business of playing golf.'

●　●　●　●

Playing golf was all Jimmy Martin ever wanted to do and all he ever knew until he passed away in 2001.

He was born in July 1924, six months before his great golfing rival Christy O'Connor. His father, James, was

'Jimmy always had his sights on playing regularly on tour, for what it was worth back then. He and I spent a lot of time going to tournaments in England and Ireland. He never drove. I always used to pick him up and take him to the events,' said Nicky.

With a game based almost entirely around his unerring ability to get up and down from 100 yards out, Jimmy carved out a successful career on tour.

'He wasn't long off the tee, but he was deadly accurate and in Bradshaw's class from 100 yards out,' added Nicky.

'The game seemed to come pretty naturally to him. He never really had to graft at it. He was a beautiful pitcher of the ball and very seldom took three to get down. With a short iron in his hand he was simply brilliant.'

> 'Jimmy was a good foursomes player. He kept the ball in play and had good nerve.'

the professional at Greystones Golf Club in Co. Wicklow and from an early age Jimmy looked destined to follow his father into the family business.

He spent six years training with his father at Greystones before moving to Sunningdale Golf Club as assistant to Arthur Lees in 1954. In 1956 he moved to Royal Wimbledon Golf Club, and a year later he became full professional at Bramley Golf Club in Gilford.

In 1958 he returned to Ireland and took up a post at Edmondstown Golf Club, but the lure of competition proved too strong and in 1961, while maintaining an attachment with Rush Golf Club, he committed himself full-time to tournament golf.

Former Ryder Cup star and renowned BBC commentator Peter Alliss supports that view, describing Jimmy as being above all, an excellent putter.

'Jimmy was a good foursomes player. He kept the ball in play and had good nerve,' said Alliss.

'He was a quiet man but he enjoyed life and was a good companion. He had the game to have been a bit more consistent, but I suppose they were different times we lived in then.'

In the 1960s while Christy O'Connor filled the role of Irish golf's poster boy, Jimmy Martin was quietly and effectively going about the business of making a decent living from tournament golf. He won the Piccadilly

Jimmy Martin pictured at Royal Birkdale ahead of the Ryder Cup (October 1965).

Jimmy Martin *(front row, extreme right)* **with the GB & I Ryder Cup team including Christy O'Connor** *(back row, second from left)* **at Royal Birkdale (October 1965).**

in 1964, the Silent Night in 1965 and the Carroll's International in 1968.

His best year was arguably 1964. He added the Blaxnit title to his Piccadilly crown, beating O'Connor in a play-off at Belfast's Shandon Park Golf Club. Christy had made one of his traditional final day charges to book his place in the play-off with a round of 69.

The betting money was naturally on O'Connor, but Jimmy, showing the quiet resolve that characterised his career, chipped in on the fourth play-off hole to claim the £400 first prize.

'Jimmy was a good battler. He never let on what his emotions were. He played within himself, plodded along and believed in just letting it happen,' said Nicky.

'In general, match play would not have been his thing. He was a strong stroke player, capable of grinding out pars mainly because of his excellent course management. He was a clever golfer.'

While match play was clearly not his forte, Jimmy was not averse to employing match play tactics when required.

'I once played Jimmy in the semifinal of the Mourne Cup,' said Nicky.

'We were playing the 10th and there was quite a large gallery following us. Jimmy was hitting first and because of the crowd all I could see was the head of a wooden club above the spectators and then the ball landing on the green.

'I remember thinking to myself, if it's a wood for him, it's a three-iron for me. I stepped up and fired my shot right over the back of the green. As we got to the green he said, "I got you there Nick." That's the sort of thing he would try and do. He would try and con you by gripping down the shaft of a four-wood.'

Jimmy's position on the 1965 Ryder Cup team was never in doubt following a string of strong performances which culminated in his victory at the Silent Night

In many ways, the Ryder Cup was a natural progression for Jimmy, following three Canada Cup appearances in 1962, 63 and 64 partnering Christy O'Connor. The two men could never have been described as great friends, but there was mutual respect.

'Jimmy said that Christy hadn't a bad shot in his bag. There was a bit of a clash of personalities, but you must remember, in that period of the 60s they were Ireland's top golfers,' said Nicky.

'I remember thinking to myself, if it's a wood for him, it's a three-iron for me.'

tournament at Moortown in Leeds. After opening with a 72, he put together a stunning second round 71 in conditions which *The Irish Times* described as 'near farcical'.

His superb round, on a day when the course was lashed by gales reaching almost 60 mph, highlighted his calm approach and shot-making ability. *The Irish Times* reported: 'Martin seemed to enjoy the buffeting and admitted afterwards, "Sometimes I wish it would blow more often at these events."'

Jimmy maintained his lead after round three but threw in a final round 74 and was caught by Welshman Dave Thomas who finished with a final round 67. The two men shared first and second place and collected £800 each, with Jimmy jumping from eighth to fifth in the Ryder Cup team table.

His form dipped after the Silent Night triumph and entering the final qualifying competition, the Esso Tournament (a match play event), he had slipped to seventh place with a points total of 885. The competition involved a series of round-robin match play encounters, and although clearly struggling with his game, he did enough to ensure his place on the team.

Christy was well on his way to achieving legendary Ryder Cup status when Jimmy joined him on the team to tackle the Americans at Birkdale.

The GB & I team was captained by Harry Weetman, who had been pardoned by the PGA following his outburst against Dai Rees in 1957 when he was left out of the final day singles during the Ryder Cup at Lindrick.

Weetman had to contend with an inexperienced line-up which included four rookies — Jimmy Martin, Jimmy Hitchcock, Lionel Platts and Peter Butler. From the outset it was clear he would be relying heavily on the experience of Christy O'Connor, Peter Alliss and Neil Coles, yet he remained confident of victory.

Speaking to journalists in late September he stated his belief that his team stood a fine chance of victory. 'Most of the boys are playing first-class golf at the moment and I wouldn't change the side even if it were picked today,' he said.

The Americans looked formidable on paper, even without Jack Nicklaus. Already a multiple major winner with one US Open title, two Masters and a PGA

Jimmy Martin at the Swallow-Penfold Tournament (May 1961).

Championship to his name, he still had to complete his PGA apprenticeship. However, the American captain Byron Nelson could call on experienced performers like Arnold Palmer, Dave Marr and Billy Casper.

'I have a well-balanced team as a whole. I know the British team will definitely be difficult. I have heard that Peter Alliss has beaten Palmer twice. Naturally you have to have respect for such a man,' said Nelson.

Nelson's confidence in his team was highlighted even before play began, when he refused to send for a replacement after Johnny Potts was ruled out through injury.

Weetman felt the decision not to send for a replacement might backfire on the visitors claiming, 'Having only nine men left and therefore being able to rest only one player each round means that some of them will have

Jimmys had suffered a heavy defeat at the hands of Alliss and O'Connor, who had finished their practice round with a better-ball score of eight under par.

It was not ideal preparation, but Weetman clearly believed in his rookie pairing. He openly declared that they would play some part in the proceedings on day one and he was true to his word.

After the teams finished the morning foursomes all square with two wins each, he pitched the two Jimmys into battle in the afternoon foursomes against Julius Boros and Tony Lema.

Boros and Lema were battle-hardened Ryder Cup competitors and had actually led off the American challenge against Lionel Platts and Peter Butler in the morning foursomes, recording a narrow one-hole victory.

> ## 'Jimmy normally took anything that happened on the golf course in his stride.'

to play in each series of the foursomes, fourballs and singles which constitute the match. They are not used to playing two rounds a day in America, and those who do could get tired.'

Weetman was conscious of the fact that his team needed to get off to a flying start if they were to put any kind of pressure on the Americans.

'It would give them (the players) a great boost to get on top right away,' he said. 'The match will be decided on the short play, especially by putting.'

In practice, Jimmy partnered fellow rookie Jimmy Hitchcock. On the Thursday prior to the match getting under way, the newspapers reported that the two

'Jimmy normally took anything that happened on the golf course in his stride, but it was different in the Ryder Cup,' said Nicky.

'He said it was the most nerve-racking thing he had ever done. He and Hitchie (Hitchcock) tossed a coin on the 1st tee to see who would hit off first and when Jimmy won the toss he let Hitchie hit off. So Hitchie fires one down the middle and when Jimmy gets to the ball he grabs the four-wood out of the bag.

'He used to say that when he put the club behind the ball, "she started to dance." Even with the club jumping about, he still managed to find the green. Hitchie slipped the first putt six feet past, but Jimmy managed to hole the one back and they were on their way.'

That putt may have settled Jimmy's nerves somewhat, but the rookie pairing struggled in the Ryder Cup cauldron. Boros and Lema won holes 3, 4 and 5 to take a stranglehold on the match and were never really troubled on their way to a 5 and 4 victory.

'Boros with his wonderful ease of movement, which makes the actual hit of the ball almost imperceptible, and the graceful Lema were far outside their opponents off the tee and exacted full punishment for any error', reported Paul MacWeeney in *The Irish Times*.

'There were unfortunately plenty. Hitchcock struck a chip from close to the 3rd green nine feet past, so that was one up to the Americans. Then Lema put his tee shot four feet past the pin at the 4th and Boros tapped in for the two.

'At the 5th, Martin pulled a pitch from the middle of the fairway into a trap beside the green and Boros holed from ten feet to go three up. There is little more to say after that, for if Martin holed a ten-footer to halve the 7th in two after another fine tee shot by Boros this time, Hitchcock could not take any of his chances from around six feet and he, in fact, was the weakest member of the party.'

On the whole, GB & I competed well on that opening day and finished level at 4-4.

'There was some tremendous golf played. If we keep breaking even and then go ahead on Saturday, I shall be satisfied,' said Weetman.

In fact, the opposite happened. The US took control on day two and swept to an emphatic 19½-12½ win.

Jimmy, after suffering that heavy defeat at the hands of Boros and Lema, was left on the sidelines for the remainder of the event.

MacWeeney felt Jimmy was unlucky not to get another outing at Birkdale. 'Finally, there was the unfortunate Martin whom Weetman erased from his calculations after he and Hitchcock had been trounced by the best American pair, Boros and Lema, in the foursomes on Thursday afternoon,' he wrote in *The Irish Times*.

'Martin had done rather more than his fair share in the task beyond the scope of the partnership and he deserved as much consideration, subsequently, as was given to Hitchcock and Platts. It was a depressing experience for him.'

Nicky Lynch agrees that the Ryder Cup was not an enjoyable time for Jimmy. 'He didn't really look back on the Ryder Cup with any great fondness. He enjoyed some parts of it, but I suppose in general he didn't think much of it,' said Nicky.

'The nerves might have been too much for him to cope with. You never heard him speak about the Ryder Cup, or the Canada Cup for that matter (Jimmy would play in the Canada Cup for the last time in 1966). He just wasn't the type of person who talked a lot about what he had achieved.

'It wouldn't surprise me if he asked not to be selected for the singles. He had qualified for the Ryder Cup and that was probably good enough for him.'

Jimmy continued to perform well on tour in the years following the Ryder Cup, but as the 1960s wore on he

> **That putt may have settled Jimmy's nerves somewhat, but the rookie pairing struggled in the Ryder Cup cauldron.**

Jimmy Martin in action during the late 1960s.

Jimmy Martin poses for the camera at the Assistant Professionals Tournament, Coombe Hill (May 1951).

became less prolific. He won the Carroll's International in Woodbrook in 1968, and in 1969 he won the Irish National Championship title at Dundalk.

As he slowly cut back on his tournament appearances, he spent more time in the pro shop at Rush, but he was clearly happiest among his peers competing on tour.

'He enjoyed tournament golf, and enjoyed the socialising involved with being on tour. Even when he had quit the main tour, he played a lot on the seniors circuit and did quite well without ever winning anything,' said Nicky.

'The thing about Jimmy was that he loved playing golf. It was more than a job to him. He played a lot of social golf and played right up until he passed away simply because he loved the game.

> **'The thing about Jimmy was that he loved playing golf. It was more than a job to him.'**

'There's a famous story told about him which tells you a lot about the type of person he was. In the early 70s Jimmy made a couple of trips to compete in Australia. One day a journalist with the *People* — I think it was Frank Johnston — met him on a train. Jimmy said hello and asked Frank if he was going to work. Frank said he was and he then asked Jimmy where he was going. Jimmy said he was off to Australia — he was carrying one small bag at the time. He said it as if he was going to Cork for a couple of days.

'That's exactly the way he was. He just quietly went about his life without any fuss and that was the way he liked it.'

Chapter 6

Hugh Boyle

Hugh Boyle playing from a bunker.

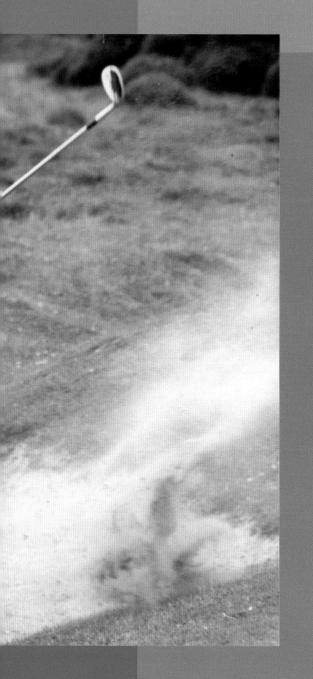

Legend has it that Ben Hogan was one of golf's most uncompromising characters. He was a tough, no-nonsense Texan who didn't suffer fools gladly.

In 1967 Hugh Boyle was making his debut in the Ryder Cup at the Champions Club in Houston, Texas, against an American side captained by Hogan.

Boyle was 31, overawed by the occasion, and just about to drive off during one of the practice days when Hogan pulled up in a cart.

'He was always dragging on a cigarette,' recalls Hugh. 'He watched us all drive off and I cheekily said to him, "Have we got you worried Mr Hogan?"

'He didn't say anything, he just dragged on the weed, looked at me with those piercing eyes and then drove off. He probably thought to himself, "Who is this prat?"'

Hugh Boyle receives the trophy from Yosaji Kobayashi, vice-president of the *Yomiuri* newspaper after winning the International Open Golf Tournament at the Yomiuri Country Club (April 1966).

The 'prat' in question was a native of Omeath who probably had more in common with Hogan than either man would ever care to admit. Hugh Boyle's career never reached the heights of Hogan's but, like the great man, he was utterly devoted to the game.

Hugh's family moved to Birmingham in 1939 and he became obsessed with the game whilst caddying at Mosley Golf Club. His pursuit of excellence took him across the world as he grafted and worked to develop a game that would allow him to compete at the highest level.

'I once watched Sam Snead and Ben Hogan practising at Wentworth whilst they were representing America in the Canada Cup (in 1956),' said Hugh.

'I was a 20-year-old assistant professional at Olton Golf Club and I travelled down with one of the members. When we got there I went straight to the range and arrived just as Hogan and Snead came out to practise. I stood there with a handful of spectators and watched two of the best players in the world go through their paces.'

That master-class left a lasting impression on Hugh. He realised he had a lot of work to do on his own swing, but he was more determined that ever to find out just how good he could be. In striving to do so, he became one of the original 'range rats', a man devoted to practice.

'As a youngster, when you're impressionable, you see people playing well, hitting it nicely and you want to emulate them,' said Hugh.

'I got hooked on the game. When I wasn't caddying I was playing. I quit playing football and would often caddie four rounds on a Saturday, two in the morning and two in the afternoon.'

Hugh moved seamlessly from caddying to working in the pro shop at Edgbaston GC at the age of 15, where he spent most of his time cleaning shoes and clubs, and learning how to repair clubs.

'There is every chance that had I done my National Service, my approach to the game and a possible career in golf would have changed, but I was lucky. I failed the medical,' admits Hugh.

When he went for his medical he was in the prime of his life. He was 21 years old, six feet two inches tall, and fit. What he didn't know was that he had a hernia.

'You know that part when they ask you to drop your trousers and cough? Well, when I did they had a little poke around and then gave me a grade four (a fail). I think they knew I wanted to be a golfer, because normally they sent you away, you had the operation and then you were called back in for another medical,' said Hugh.

That bit of good fortune ensured that Hugh remained committed to the game. He was single, practising diligently, and Great Britain and Ireland were about

What drove him on was a burning desire to become good enough to maybe, someday, win a tournament.

He claims he never had dreams of winning the Open, and his Ryder Cup aspirations didn't appear until later on in his career. What drove him on was a burning desire to become good enough to maybe, someday, win a tournament.

He left Edgbaston GC after 18 months and moved to Olton GC to work as assistant to professional Tom Collinge. By that time he was playing off scratch and whilst at Olton he won the professional section of the Youths' Championship.

He never had an amateur career by which to gauge his own ability, so those early forays into the professional arena gave him an idea of just how his game was progressing. He was certain he had taken the right career path. The problem was, National Service was looming.

to do the unthinkable by taking back the Ryder Cup at Lindrick. Hugh had always been aware of the contest and its great players, but it took the Lindrick triumph for the contest to really register with him.

'I remember reading every paper I could get my hands on to find out as much as I could. All the best players competed in the Ryder Cup, but at 21 it seemed a long way off to me,' said Hugh.

It took ten more years for Hugh to force his way on to the team — years of hard work and relentless practice.

Hugh's fledging career took him from Olton to the Berkshire Golf Club near Ascot and from there he took up an attachment at Coombe Hill Golf Club as assistant to former Open champion Dick Burton.

While Burton encouraged Hugh to believe in his own ability, Hugh developed a more competitive edge on the golf course, playing in the company of Neil Coles, Ken Bousfield and Tony Grubb. He also spent four winters away teaching, first in Hong Kong and then in Pakistan.

The money he earned on those trips gave him some financial stability. Without having to worry about where the next pound was coming from, he was able to compete more regularly on the tour.

'Thinking about it now, it was a long road, but that's just the way it was back then. I always felt I was improving

The success continued in the winter of 1966 when, through the patronage of Birmingham FC vice-president David Wiseman, Hugh competed on the Far East circuit and created a bit of history by becoming the first European to win in Japan when he won the Yomiuri Open in Tokyo. He returned to England as a proven winner and underlined his ability by claiming the Daks Tournament at Wentworth.

Featuring strongly on the order of merit and with his confidence at an all-time high, Hugh's thoughts began to turn to the Ryder Cup and the possibility of making his debut.

'I came back from my last stint in Pakistan in 1964 and spent the summer on tour without making any impact.'

during those years, and whilst I wasn't winning I was picking up the necessary experience,' said Hugh.

'I came back from my last stint in Pakistan in 1964 and spent the summer on tour without making any impact. But in 1965 things began to go well and I started putting some scores together.'

Hugh finished seventh in the Yorkshire Evening News event, 12th in the Open at Birkdale and secured his biggest cheque with a second place finish at the Senior Service event at Dalmahoy.

He can't really put his finger on why things started to click for him in 1965. 'I think I was just getting there,' he said.

'Golf is a game of dedication, of keeping at it, and I was single and dedicated. It had been a long learning curve for me, but it was just a matter of opportunity and time at it.'

'1967 was a Ryder Cup year and there was an added buzz around the events. I hadn't gone back to the Far East circuit in the winter of 1966, but had sorted out an attachment at John Jacobs' driving range at Sandown Park. I practised hard during the winter and came out to see what I could achieve in 1967,' he said.

The selection process for the 1967 matches was simple: the top 12 on the order of merit were to be chosen to represent GB & I. As the season progressed, Hugh played consistently without finding the winner's enclosure. He made a couple of successful raids in Ireland, but his best finish in counting events was a second in the PGA Championship.

It all came down to the final qualifying event, the Open at Hoylake, which was won by Roberto de Vicenzo.

'Three of us were going for the last two places — Peter Butler, George Will and I. Butler missed the cut and

Hugh Boyle tees off at the start of the final round of the International Open Golf Tournament at the Yomiuri Country Club (April 1966).

that automatically ensured that Will and I made it,' said Hugh.

'I had been nervous going into the event, but I was confident in my own ability. I was playing well and I finished strongly with rounds of 70 and 68. I was really chuffed to make the team. You get fitted out for a new suit, you get a new bag, new gear. It was a big thing for me.'

It was a huge personal achievement for Hugh. Never fully convinced of his own ability, he rose to the occasion and performed superbly under pressure. It

was, however, nothing like the pressure he was going to feel at the Ryder Cup, and the enormity of the event hit home when the plane carrying the GB & I team touched down in Houston a few days ahead of the tournament.

'They had a motorcade to take us from the airport to the hotel,' said Hugh. 'There were police outriders, the works — you know how the Americans can go over the top. I was a rookie and it was completely overpowering.'

Hugh Boyle plays from the rough during the News of the World Championship at Walton Heath (September 1967).

He was one of three rookies on the team, the others being Malcolm Gregson who won the order of merit in 1967 and Tony Jacklin. Aside from being a Ryder Cup novice, Hugh was also something of a match play rookie. He readily admits that he had little experience of the one-on-one form of the game.

'I knew what it was like to have to make four on the last to win. I knew what it felt like and at that stage in my career I knew how to do it,' he said.

'That's one of the reasons I worked so hard on my game. The last nine holes on a Sunday afternoon — there's nothing like it. That's why you do it.'

The rest of the GB & I team were very experienced. Three of them, Dave Thomas, Peter Alliss and Christy O'Connor had played in six previous contests. GB & I also had the fiercely combative Welshman Dai Rees as captain.

A veteran of nine Ryder Cups and renowned as the captain who beat the Americans at Lindrick, the enthusiastic Rees was installed in a bid to stoke up some patriotic fervour in the visiting side.

In contrast, Ben Hogan had a relatively inexperienced outfit. The US had four first-timers, and their best player, Jack Nicklaus, still wasn't eligible to compete. Nevertheless, the Americans were clear favourites.

The general feeling, even among some of the GB & I team, was that the best they could hope for was a damage-limitation exercise. Certainly the rookie Irishman, eager to get a crack at the Americans, felt there was an air of resignation among some members of the team.

'I think there was a feeling among some of them that we were going to get beaten. I think some of the older players had got used to being beaten,' said Hugh.

'They were pretty resigned to it when they travelled to America. Let's face it, we didn't have that many players who played in the States. I can't think of any. It's not like now. We didn't have young players competing all over the world. I had never played in America. We weren't used to it.'

Practice went well in the lead-up to the event, with Rees working hard to build confidence among the team.

'He was very dynamic and hated losing to the Americans. I knew him from the circuit and we got on reasonably well together,' said Hugh.

'I had no problems with him throughout the match. He kept us informed, tried to keep us going. You realised that with all his experience he knew what he was doing. He was someone that I looked up to. He was a good captain and managed to go about his business without going over the top.'

The Champions course provided little concern for the GB & I side. It was very similar to the parkland courses at home. It was, however, long for the era at over 7,000 yards and had a number of huge sweeping greens. It was tree lined, the fairways were tight and, according to Hugh, the turf itself was cut quite tight.

'I think there was a feeling among some of them that we were going to get beaten. I think some of the older players had got used to being beaten.'

It was this fact that led most of the team to plump for the choice of the small ball over the larger US version. The selection of which ball to use seems to have been the most taxing question for the players in the build-up to the matches. According to Hugh, the team practised with both but ultimately they decided to stick with what they knew best.

'I had had some experience of the larger ball from playing in Hong Kong. In the end we were all so used to it (the smaller ball) that it would have been a big change to switch with only four days' practice,' said Hugh.

The Americans had no such problems about which product to use. Ben Hogan decreed early on that they would play with the British version, despite some rumblings of discontent from Arnold Palmer.

Rees mixed and matched the pairings during practice, but Hugh felt from early on that he had already settled on a number of tried and tested pairings. Coles and

together. I had a notion that at some stage we would play together in a match, and I was happy with that. He was our No. 1 player that year.'

Hugh's assessment was right. He and Gregson were left out of the opening morning foursomes but were told by Rees that they would be playing in the afternoon.

With the morning off, the rookie pairing had time to watch some of the opening matches and play a few holes. It did little for their nerves, however, and Hugh claims that he has never been as nervous as when he stood on the 1st tee for their opening match against Arnold Palmer and Gardner Dickinson, who had already enjoyed a 2 and 1 morning victory over O'Connor and Alliss.

The inexperienced GB & I pairing found themselves in the middle of a whirlwind as the two Americans, buoyed by their morning success and in front of Arnold's huge crowd, got off to a blistering start.

'But you know, it's a team and the captain makes his choices. I was fairly open about whom I was paired with.'

Bernard Hunt looked inseparable, as did O'Connor and Peter Alliss. That ruled out any chance of an all-Irish partnership, which was disappointing for Hugh.

'Christy did say at one stage that he would like to have played with me (the two men would go on to represent Ireland in the Canada Cup a month later),' said Hugh.

'But you know, it's a team and the captain makes his choices. I was fairly open about whom I was paired with. I felt I was one of the team and they were all good players.

'I played a bit with Malcolm Gregson. He was more my age and as a fellow newcomer we both got on well

'It really was a case of welcome to the Ryder Cup,' said Hugh.

'They were out in 31 (par 36) and we were five down after nine. Palmer gave Dickinson the line on every green and he just knocked it in the hole. We managed to grab a couple of holes back coming home, but they eventually beat us 5 and 4.

'It was a baptism of fire. Malcolm and I played reasonably well. We went to the turn in level par, but we faced a barrage of birdies and we couldn't match them.'

Hugh Boyle in action.

Hugh Boyle pictured at the Swallow-Penfold Tournament (May 1961).

The visitors finished day one trailing 5-2, and Hugh remembers the feeling of disappointment in the team room. The annoying thing was that a number of the matches had gone to the 17th and 18th.

'I was probably a bit shell-shocked, to be honest. It all happens so fast. You tee off and suddenly you're five down at the turn. I just wanted to get to bed. It had been a long day, almost 12 hours including travel to and from the hotel,' said Hugh.

Hugh maintains that Rees stayed positive and his approach did lift their spirits as the team looked forward to having another go at the Americans on day two. Once again Rees left Hugh out of the morning session as he sought to cut into the American lead.

Instead, the GB & I side ran into an American brick wall. The US, without Arnold Palmer who was rested by Hogan, swept the four morning matches.

With the cup almost out of his grasp, Rees desperately juggled his pairings about for the afternoon and Hugh

opponents over the front nine. When George eagled the 9th, GB & I were four up and had gone out in a better-ball score of 30. A win looked on the cards, but as they turned for home their grip on the match began to slacken.

The 10th at the Champions course was a 448 yard par four. Standing in the middle of the fairway and with George already on the green in two, Hugh debated his options.

'The green was double tiered and the pin was tucked away on the right of the top tier,' said Hugh.

'George and I talked about what I should do. We knew that if I missed it right I was dead, but he was already on the green. I went for the flag and, unfortunately, missed it right. It was down to George and he three-putted up the slope. The Americans won the hole in par and I think that was the turning point.'

On the 11th Hugh's birdie putt lipped out, while Palmer holed his to cut the deficit to just two. On the 230 yard par three 12th, Palmer hit a long iron in close to the flag, but

'I was probably a bit shell-shocked, to be honest. It all happens so fast. You tee off and suddenly you're five down at the turn.'

found himself paired with George Will in the last fourball of the day.

Will was older than Hugh and had played on the 1963 and 65 teams. 'George's experience definitely helped, especially as we got a tough draw against Palmer and Julius Boros,' said Hugh.

With nothing to lose, George and Hugh blitzed their

Hugh responded with a fine iron and the hole was halved in three. The momentum was clearly with the Americans and they won the 13th and 14th to level the match.

'The crowd were absolutely hysterical at this stage. They had fought back and Palmer was playing like a god, but we managed to hang in there. George played well at that stage because, to be honest, I lost the plot for a few holes,' admitted Hugh.

Hugh Boyle drives off during the Assistant Professionals Tournament at Coombe Hill (May 1954).

It was dark when the group reached the 18th tee, with the match all square. 'It was very gloomy as we played the last. It was a difficult par four at the best of times, but standing on the tee George couldn't see the fairway,' said Hugh.

'When I was standing in the fairway waiting to hit my second, I couldn't see the green. George made it clear that he didn't think we should finish, but the officials were adamant that we should finish the match.'

The pressure was now on Hugh as George had found a fairway bunker off the tee and could not reach the green in two.

'I had a two-iron in my hand but cut it away to the right of the green. I hit a good chip and had eight to ten feet for a par, but I missed it,' said Hugh.

'George also finished with a five and the Americans won the hole with a four. I was devastated. Both George and I were in an awful state afterwards. To be four up on Palmer and throw it away — it was terrible. I was gobsmacked.'

Reflecting on their decision to play the last in the gathering gloom, Hugh feels that both he and Will should have stood their ground.

'If we had been a bit more experienced, we would have insisted that we come back the next day to finish the match. It wouldn't happen today. The captain would be called and he would make the decision,' he said.

Hugh's black mood was reflected by the whole team as they looked back on a disastrous day. From the eight matches played, GB & I had gathered just half a point.

They trailed by 13-3 and the Ryder Cup was surely out of their reach.

There was no way back for the visitors and even their irrepressible captain knew it would take a miracle in the singles for GB & I to win.

Some early morning fog delayed the start of the singles on day three, and Hugh found himself starting from the 10th tee against Texas boy Gay Brewer.

'He knew the course well and banged in two early birdies to lead by two holes. I thought to myself, here

'It was a wonderful experience. I wouldn't have missed it for the world. The team got on well together, but it would have been nice to give them a better match.'

From the Ryder Cup, Hugh went on to Palm Springs for a break before joining up with Christy O'Connor in Mexico City for the Canada Cup.

He got married to Rosalind in 1970, and continued to play on the tour before settling down to a club job. He retired from his position as professional at Royal Wimbledon Golf Club in 2002.

'That's the experience I have had and it's nice. That's why I've always been grateful that I got in.'

we go again, but I hung in there and I was only one down at the turn,' said Hugh.

But Hugh's fight back only served to put off the inevitable, and Brewer rammed in three birdies in the next five holes to win 4 and 3.

That proved to be the end of Hugh's Ryder Cup experience. He was offered the chance to play in the afternoon singles but declined in favour of Neil Coles, who went on to complete a morning and afternoon double over Doug Sanders.

In the end it proved to be a disappointing debut. Hugh had nothing to show from his three matches except the knowledge that he had let a golden opportunity slip away.

'I was quite happy with my overall play. Apart from the back nine holes against Palmer and Boros, I competed well,' said Hugh.

Hugh never managed to force his way back on to the team, although he did come close in 1971.

'I hoped to get in but it never happened. I really enjoyed it but it wasn't something I aimed for,' he said.

'You must always remember, it was about earning a living. If it had come along again, it would have been a bonus. But I did make it, and once you're a Ryder Cup player, you're always a Ryder Cup player. People always remember you for it. It stays with you.

'That's the experience I have had and it's nice. That's why I've always been grateful that I got in. The only regret I have is that we didn't hang on to get something out of Arnold Palmer. That's the one that got away.'

Chapter 7

Eddie Polland

Eddie Polland pictured at the Senior British Open Championship, Royal County Down Golf Club (July 2000).

In January 1970, Eddie Polland jumped at an offer to play in a Pro-Am in Florida. It was a fantastic opportunity for the 23-year-old assistant professional. He could put in some serious practice away from the cold and damp of Belfast and his base at Balmoral Golf Club. As an added incentive, the trip offered him the possibility of glimpsing the world's best golfer, Jack Nicklaus.

Eddie Polland playing from a bunker.

'A few miles down the road from where I was staying, there was a golf club which Nicklaus was attached to,' said Eddie.

'I went down one day to see if I could just get a little look — just to see what he looked like, even. Of course, he wasn't there. I went into the shop and the assistant explained that Nicklaus was rarely there, that he just used it as a base, but he invited me in and showed me around Jack's office. I couldn't believe how many spare bags full of golf clubs he had. There must have been 20 tournament bags jammed full of clubs.'

The assistant explained that Jack was sent all the latest equipment and that he tried every single club sent to him.

'I was amazed. I had never seen so many clubs in my life! Even then, Jack was ahead of the game, testing and looking at new equipment,' said Eddie.

'I lifted one of the clubs lying against the table. Did he use this one? I asked. "Yeah," said the assistant, "that's the new Hogan sand wedge." I told him it was unbelievable, that we didn't get stuff like that back at home.

'So he says, "Here, take it. Jack has tried it and he doesn't use it, so take it with you."

'I met Jack a couple of years later and explained the story of how his assistant had given me one of his wedges. I was playing against him in the Ryder Cup fourballs at Muirfield (1973) and found myself in one of the deep greenside bunkers on the par four 3rd.

'I went in with Jack's wedge in my hand and played a lovely shot close to the hole. As I was getting out of the bunker, Jack shouted across at me: "I want my sand wedge back."

'He didn't get it. He's a good friend, but I've still got the wedge.'

• • • •

Eddie Polland was born to play golf.

'I still remember being in school and whenever the teacher would ask us to write about what we wanted to be when we grew up, instead of saying a fireman I always wrote down I wanted to be a golf professional,' he said.

He joined the Mourne Golf Club and soon carved out a reputation as an exceptional young player.

'Golf came very naturally to me. Whenever I was playing, say on a Saturday, I would always have people watching me. I could never really understand it,' said Eddie.

'They never said anything, they just wandered around. I used to say to myself, do these people have no work to go to? It never really dawned on me that they were out to watch me play. As I got a bit older people would say, "One day, you're going to be a professional golfer."'

No one disputed this assertion, least of all Eddie, who was soon learning the golf trade under the watchful eye of Newcastle professional, Ian Murdock. 'Ian was a wonderful man. I was in my early teens at the time, and during the summer and after school he taught me

'I could have played at senior level, but the problem was I couldn't afford it. I always felt a bit peeved about it.'

Born in Newcastle, Co. Down, in 1947, Eddie grew up less than 100 metres from the 15th tee at Royal County Down.

'Golf is in the family, although no one in my immediate family plays,' he said. 'My uncle John was the greenkeeper at Royal County Down for 49 years. His brother Willie was the professional at Lahinch, and Willie's son Robert is currently the professional at Lahinch.

'There were always golf clubs around the house. As a child I would ask for a bike for my birthday, but Willie would make me a golf club. I used to hop over the fence and play on the course.'

how to fix shafts, regrip clubs, that sort of thing,' adds Eddie.

His amateur career flourished at the Mourne club. He was runner-up in the Leinster Boys in 1965 and went on to represent Ireland at Boys level in 1965, 66 and 67.

'I could have played at senior level, but the problem was I couldn't afford it. I always felt a bit peeved about it. My mum and dad didn't have a lot of money and I didn't feel right about taking it to play golf,' he said.

'I did a bit of caddying to make some money and I also worked at the local hotel, but in the end I knew that if I wanted to continue playing golf seriously I had to turn professional.'

It wasn't a difficult decision to make, and at 21 years of age Eddie Polland shocked no one when he turned his back on amateur golf and embarked on a professional career which is still going strong today, some 37 years later. Despite a string of serious injuries, particularly to his back and elbow, he continues to play regularly on the European Seniors Tour. When the season comes to a close, he returns to his base in Spain, where he has a thriving property business.

Eddie attributes his longevity primarily to the type of golfer he is. He describes himself as a 'hands and arms' golfer, a player who relies on feel instead of mechanics.

However, some of that endurance must surely be the result of his close association with the late, great Fred Daly. Fred was the ultimate competitor and, similarly, Eddie loves to be in the thick of the action.

'Anything I ever won had Fred Daly's name on it,' he said.

'I'm standing in Belfast in the rain trying to work out where I'm supposed to go, and I see a bus with Balmoral on it. I suddenly thought, Fred Daly's at Balmoral. I'll go there. I walked into the clubhouse at Balmoral and found Fred standing in the bar playing one of the fruit machines.

'I was supposed to start a job today with Billy Robinson, but I changed my mind and came here,' I said. Fred asked me who I was and I told him my name was Eddie Polland. He asked me was I any good and I told him I was brilliant.

'He then asked me why I hadn't gone on to Belvoir and I said, why go to Billy Robinson when you are the best. No one has a record as good as yours.

'As soon as I said that, he welcomed me in and from that day until he died, we were really good friends.'

Eddie was attached to Balmoral for some 14 years.

'It gave me great confidence. He told me many times that I would play in the Ryder Cup. I took it all for granted.'

Eddie's one and only club job was as assistant to Ireland's only Open Championship winner and it came about purely as a result of some good fortune and his innate self-confidence.

'My father knew about my plans to turn professional and he sorted out a job for me with Billy Robinson, the pro at Belvoir Park Golf Club in Belfast,' added Eddie.

'The thing was, that when I got on the bus to go to Belfast to see Billy, I didn't know which stop to get off at and I ended up in the middle of the city without a clue about how I was going to get to Belvoir.

'I never wanted to go anywhere else. I never wanted to leave Fred. He wasn't a mentor, he was my friend and he was a great guy to know,' said Eddie.

'You know, I never once got any tuition from Fred. I would say to him come out and watch me hit a few balls. I would hit some iron shots and ask him what he thought. "Great," he'd say. I'd ask him about my grip, my stance. "First class," he'd say. So eventually I'd ask him what I needed to do, and he'd say, "Nothing."

'There would be times when the press would ring him for a quote, and he would always tell them about the great assistant he had. But he never saw me play; he only watched me hit balls.

'It gave me great confidence. He told me many times that I would play in the Ryder Cup. I took it all for granted. In my mind, all I had to do was go out and play.'

Buoyed by Fred's words of encouragement, Eddie set out on his tournament career but struggled to translate his ball-striking ability into consistent scoring.

'At the end of the 1960s and the beginning of the 70s, I started off by playing in a few events,' added Eddie.

'I'd be playing with guys and they'd be shooting 69 to my 72, and I couldn't work out why because I knew I

was striking the ball better. I had to learn how to score, had to develop a competitive edge and, remember, when I was starting out it was hard work.

'There were some world-class operators out there, people like Coles, Huggett, Butler, Alliss, Bousfield. I worked it out, cut out the silly mistakes, learned how to score. No matter who I played with, I always thought to myself I can play better than them.'

Eddie's development was helped in those early years by the regular sorties he made to play on the Sunshine Tour in South Africa.

'That was great for me,' he said. 'I was very lucky. Even from an early age when I was in Northern Ireland I was always offered fantastic sponsorship. I never had to pay

Eddie Polland plays from the rough during the Ryder Cup at Muirfield (September 1973).

Eddie Polland guides a putt towards the hole during the Ryder Cup at Muirfield (September 1973).

any of my expenses. I learnt a lot during those three to four months of the year I spent in South Africa.'

Eddie continued to make steady progress and claimed his first title of any note in 1971 at the Parmeco Classic in Nottingham. It was a low-key event but it proved to the young pro that he could compete with the top players and win.

From that winning platform his career took off. He got married, bought a house in Belfast and started a family. He featured strongly in the order of merit and cemented his place in the top ranks of the tour by winning the Penfold-Bournemouth Tournament in 1973, effectively sealing his place on the Ryder Cup team.

'I remember playing in the Benson and Hedges in York when Dai Rees came up and had a word with me,' said Eddie.

Eddie, Rees ensured that the question of 'form' was not an issue with the man from Belfast.

In fact, the option to drop players was never used, and the top 12 point scorers were selected for the matches which would be played in Scotland for the first time. Eddie was pleased to make the team but not overly excited at the prospect of taking on the Americans.

'You must always remember, it was nothing like the Ryder Cup of today. It was a three-day event every couple of years against the Americans,' he said.

'It's only when you become involved in it that you realise how big and how important it is to you. Not the team — to you. You can see it now — everybody wants to play Ryder Cup. Really, I don't know now whether it is better to win a tournament or play in the Ryder Cup.

> ### 'You must always remember, it was nothing like the Ryder Cup of today.'

'He told me I had to put in a good strong effort with the Ryder Cup coming up. "You're definitely going to be in, but it would look better for you and suit me much better if you could go out and shoot a low number," he said.

'I played well in the tournament and shot something around 65 on the last day. I think I eagled the last to do it. I finished in the top ten, making sure of my place. Everybody was happy.'

Rees's pep-talk probably had its basis in the selection process the PGA had put in place for the 1973 matches. In the British system the 12 top point scorers in tournament play were automatically chosen. However, the selectors had an option to omit two or three players in favour of men in form. By having a quiet word with

'Back then the Open Championship was everything. It was like Wimbledon. The Ryder Cup wasn't very high profile or prestigious. You weren't really catered for; you even had to make your own way there!'

On the positive side, Eddie was taking another step along the way of emulating Fred Daly.

'We used to talk about the Ryder Cup. During the winter, when the weather was bad and there was no one around, we'd go into the clubhouse, make some tea and sit down for a chat,' added Eddie.

'He would talk about the great players, how he competed against them, how he coped with playing in the cup. I got the inside track which was great.'

The GB & I team which gathered at Muirfield saw two changes to the side that had been defeated in St Louis, Missouri, in 1971. Two rookies, Eddie and Clive Clark replaced Peter Townsend and Harry Bannerman.

Christy O'Connor Snr, playing in his tenth and final Ryder Cup, was the most experienced member of either side, while captain Bernard Hunt could also call on the services of former Open winner, Tony Jacklin.

had only two days of practice. This concerned Burke who was conscious of the fact that apart from the 'superstars' of his team, some of the US players had little experience of playing on a links course.

'I wish I had come over here when I was playing competitively,' he said. 'I think I could have done well. But it's not a course you can learn in two days. I think we should have given ourselves more time.'

'Match play to me was really about playing the course. I rarely considered playing the opponent.'

Hunt was confident of victory and voiced his opinion that the young American players hardly 'had a decent swing among them'. He felt that the use of the big ball in Britain since 1968 meant that his players could play as well as the Americans. He was also aware that British players were becoming more 'international' and were competing well around the globe.

The Americans were captained by Jack Burke Jnr, remembered in Britain as the man who last lost the cup as US captain of the 1957 team at Lindrick. Burke, well aware of his reputation, joked that if things went badly he wouldn't be allowed to return home.

'The responsibility of this job is terrible,' he said. 'We're supposed to win and if you don't, don't come home. I think it's an awful job myself.'

He had four rookies on his team: British Open champion Tom Weiskopf, Homero Blancas, Chi Chi Rodriguez and Lou Graham. That inexperience was offset by the backbone of the team, Nicklaus, Palmer, Trevino and Casper.

Things didn't get off to a good start for the Americans who arrived late after a mix-up with travel plans and

This view was in stark contrast to Eddie, who was relishing the opportunity of playing at Muirfield, a course he had never competed on before. Brought up on the links at Royal County Down, he knew all about the vagaries of links golf and was comfortable in the match play environment.

'Match play to me was really about playing the course. I rarely considered playing the opponent,' said Eddie.

'Whatever he did, he did. I always felt, even from an early age, that my life would revolve around the stroke play form of the game. So for me, the best way to approach match play was as a stroke play event.'

The rookie was keen to get at the Americans, but he was acutely aware that his game was more suited to the fourballs and singles format of the contest. 'The biggest disappointment for me about the Ryder Cup was that I was basically an individual. To be honest with you, I'm a one-man show and I was only really interested in playing in the singles,' said Eddie.

Instead, Eddie found himself paired with Maurice Bembridge in the opening morning foursomes, out last against America's top pair, Jack Nicklaus and Arnold

Eddie Polland celebrates victory in the Spanish Open Championship (1976).

Palmer. Bembridge had already played on the 1969 and 71 teams and the two men knew each other well from the tour.

'I got on well with Maurice,' said Eddie. 'We shared a lot of the same interests and shared a lot of hotels together.'

However, the decision to put this untried pairing out on the opening day still baffles Eddie.

'There were a lot of very experienced players on that team and I could never understand why Bembridge and I played in the anchor match,' added Eddie. 'They (GB & I selectors) knew bloody well that Nicklaus and

Palmer were going to be paired together. I thought they'd have gone with an experienced pair.'

Looking back, it's doubtful whether any partnership would have matched the Americans. Nicklaus and Palmer simply overpowered their opponents. They went to the turn in 33 shots and were six up at the 11th before eventually going on to win 6 and 5.

'There was a lot of inexperience on our part. We tried to play negative golf, keep the ball down the fairway,' added Eddie.

'But the more we tried to do that, the more we missed it. There were times when I was hitting a three-wood

Eddie Polland lets fly with a drive at the AGFA Colour Golf Match in Slough (May 1968).

a fairway, Bembridge was up to his ears in the rough — all you could see was his pipe.

'He told me he had never been off the fairway so many times in his life! If someone had asked me, I would have explained that I preferred to play fourball and singles, but being a rookie, I was in no position to speak up.'

Despite the disappointing start for Eddie, it proved to be a good day for the GB & I side. They won the morning foursomes 2½-1½ and then consolidated

that position by winning the afternoon fourballs 3-1.

Captain Hunt declared himself 'happy but not surprised. I kept saying all along that I had a good team at heart,' he said.

Eddie was rested for that series of matches and was also left out of the morning foursomes on

when the driver was my normal shot. If I'd been in the singles or the fourballs I wouldn't have been playing that type of shot.

'The thing about foursomes is you're always thinking of your partner, trying to keep him in play. I always found that very restrictive. I mean, every time I missed

day two which GB & I split 2-2 to maintain their lead over the Americans.

He got his chance again when he was selected for the afternoon fourballs on day two, paired with the other GB & I rookie Clive Clark against Jack Nicklaus and Tom Weiskopf.

Jack Burke, faced with the possibility of losing twice on British soil, had called a team meeting after the morning foursomes on day two, at which he was forced to lay down the law. The Americans committed themselves to winning all four afternoon matches and Arnold Palmer, who had been scheduled to take a rest, replaced Lou Graham in the line-up.

With their minds firmly on the task in hand, the Americans were quickly out of the blocks — none more so than Nicklaus and Weiskopf. In their first seven holes the Americans carded five 3's but were still only two up after 11.

Eddie, who suddenly found himself as the senior partner, and Clark played well to hang on to their opponents during this early blitz.

hammering to retain the trophy. Hunt had juggled his line-up after the morning mauling, but despite many of the team complaining about being tired, and Bernard Gallacher playing whilst suffering from food poisoning, he still left Eddie on the sidelines.

'I suppose the captain's attitude was that I had played in the foursomes and fourballs and lost both. I was disappointed. I didn't ask and I didn't have any choice, so I didn't get involved,' said Eddie.

'It didn't really worry me at the back of it all because, as I say, I saw it as just another three-day event.'

Eddie never made it on to another Ryder Cup team, but he continued to make an impact in team and match play golf during the 1970s. In 1975 he won the Sun

> **'It was great to be playing my own ball again. I was raring to go and played well, grabbed a few birdies.'**

'It was great to be playing my own ball again. I was raring to go and played well, grabbed a few birdies,' said Eddie.

'Not that it made much difference — Nicklaus and Weiskopf were just phenomenal. Their figures were incredible.'

The Americans won the 12th to go three up and then halved the next four holes to close out the match 3 and 2. It was a similar story in the other matches, with the US sweeping the afternoon series to level the match at 8-8 at the end of day two. The tide had turned, and with confidence restored the US team threw themselves into the singles matches on day three.

They won the morning series 5½-2½ and drove home their advantage in the afternoon with another 5½-2½

Alliance PGA Match Play title and quickly followed that up by claiming the Irish equivalent.

He also represented Ireland six times at the World Cup and enjoyed successful outings as a member of three winning Hennessey Cognac Cup teams in 1974, 76 and 78.

'The thing about selection is that the process only comes around every other year. You can be up one year and down the next. If you're unlucky, that's Ryder Cup year,' he said.

'It was and still is a great honour to be part of the Ryder Cup. I made a lot of friends through it and I have managed to capitalise on the experience.'

Chapter 8

John O'Leary

John O'Leary blasts out of a bunker (*c*.1970).

John O'Leary should hate the Ryder Cup.

After all, this is a man who, by his own admission, half-shanked his approach shot to the 1st green during the 1975 Ryder Cup at Laurel Valley, Pennsylvania. He played four matches and lost all four as GB & I were remorselessly hammered by an American side featuring seven major champions.

It would be entirely understandable if his attitude to the biennial contest was ambivalent at best. In fact, the opposite is true. John O'Leary is a Ryder Cup devotee; he can't get it out of his system.

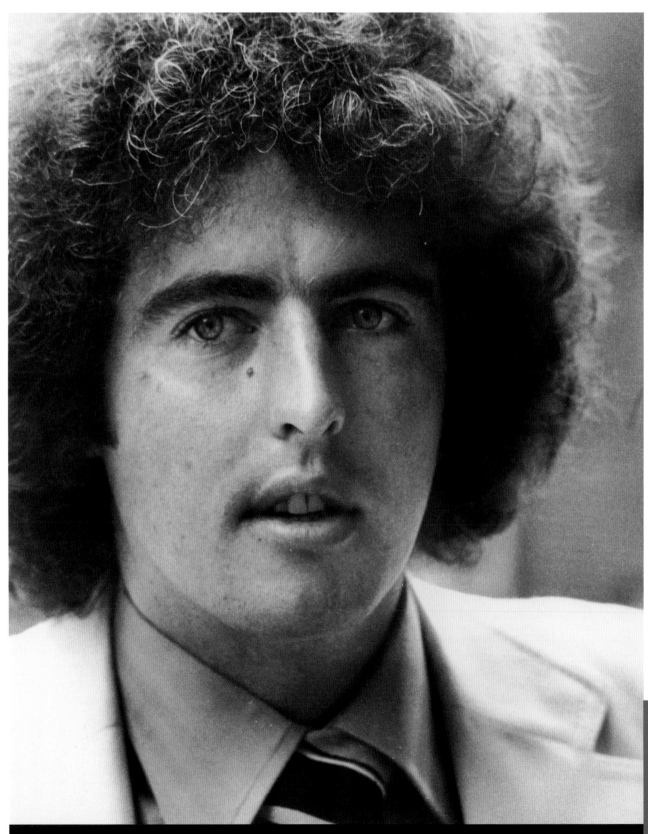

John O'Leary (May 1975).

As a founding member of the European Tour and a member of the Ryder Cup committee, John O'Leary knows just how important the Ryder Cup has always been to people on this side of the Atlantic.

As an Irishman, he is immensely proud that the event is finally coming to Ireland and he's convinced it will be a weekend to remember.

'The Irish fans are going to have some party. Irish sports fans are very special. Bernhard Langer remarked on the fact during the 2004 event at Oakland Hills,' he said.

'I still travel to Ireland a lot for rugby and soccer games. It's a real proper sports atmosphere. Everybody is on an equal footing and everybody has their own opinion. It's going to be fantastic.'

● ● ● ●

Long before Darren Clarke, John O'Leary was the flamboyant character of Irish golf with a penchant for colourful attire. He enjoyed 20 years on tour and his defining moment came in 1982 when he won the Carroll's Irish Open at Portmarnock.

His first experience of golf came as a 12 year old during a family holiday to Butlin's. A keen sportsman, he loved team sports and excelled at rugby and cricket.

'The great thing about Butlin's was that the sports events were always organised and I simply went down to try golf one day,' said John. 'They had their own nine-hole course and I got hooked. I spent the rest of the holiday there.'

When he returned from holiday, John's parents arranged some lessons with professional Adam Whiston Jnr at Dun Laoghaire Golf Club. He continued to play team sports during the school term and spent the summer on the course as a member of Foxrock Golf Club.

By the time he was 16, John was a scratch golfer and had embarked on a high-profile amateur career which brought him to the brink of Walker Cup selection.

'I left school at 18 and I stopped playing cricket and rugby at that stage,' said John. 'I was playing top-level amateur golf and wanted to avoid any injuries.'

He competed for Ireland in the Home Internationals in 1969 and 70, and was also part of the Irish team which won the European Amateur Team Golf Championship in 1969.

He was a serious contender for the 1971 Walker Cup matches at St Andrews, but was eventually overlooked by the selectors. That decision forced John's hand and he immediately turned professional.

'At the time I was uncertain about turning professional. My aim had been to make the Walker Cup team,' said John.

'It was probably helpful in a way (not to make the team) because if I had been selected, I may not have turned professional at all.'

His concerns about making the move into the paid ranks were tempered slightly by his close association with the legendary John Jacobs, the father of the European Tour.

'At the time I was uncertain about turning professional. My aim had been to make the Walker Cup team.'

'John Jacobs had a huge influence on me both as a player and a person,' said O'Leary. 'I met him for the first time when I was 14 at his golf centre in Leopardstown Race Course. Every time he was over, he would take some time to work with me on my game.

'I was the only player John ever managed and it was through him that I was able to spend the first six months of my professional career in America working with Bob Toski.'

'I had no struggles financially; I made some money from the start. In those days, by making the cut you didn't have to pre-qualify the next week. You get on a roll, make a few cuts, become exempt. It was great.'

The rookie pro certainly made a big impact in his first year, partnering Jimmy Kinsella as the Irish representatives in the 1972 World Cup in Australia and finishing second to Gary Player in the South African Masters.

'People talk today about the Ryder Cup being nothing like it was in the past and that is correct.'

Under Toski, the doyen of golf instructors, John made the transition from talented amateur to professional golfer. 'It was simply about preparing me to play and compete as a professional,' said John. 'It was invaluable.'

John returned from the US in the spring of 1972, bought a flat in Richmond, near Heathrow, and moved seamlessly into life on tour.

'Right from the start I loved it. I made some lifelong friends, people like Jack Newton, Ian Stanley, Bob Shearer and Selwyn Nathan,' he said.

More importantly, he immediately found his feet at the business end, out on the golf course.

'Some of the other players took five or six years to feel they had any game. I was straight in the first week. It's funny in hindsight,' he said.

'In my first event at South Herts I holed a 20 foot putt on the last green to qualify for the last two rounds. I then made the cut the next week and the week after that. If I had missed that 20 footer, who knows what would have happened.

Firmly established on tour, John was able to devote himself to achieving his golfing ambitions — win the Open Championship, win the Irish Open and, of course, compete in the Ryder Cup.

'People talk today about the Ryder Cup being nothing like it was in the past and that is correct in one sense. Television today is superb. Every shot, every hole of every match is broadcast. It's fantastic,' said John.

'Some of my friends, many of them not even golfers, say it's the best sports event of the year. They sit down for three days and get lost in it.

'I think the Ryder Cup has always been huge to us because of the dominance of the US teams over the years. The Ryder Cup has always been massive on this side of the Atlantic. Just look at Lindrick in 1957. The crowds were absolutely incredible.

'For me personally, the 1969 Ryder Cup at Birkdale was a sensation, the famous halved match. I was still in Dublin at the time. It was an incredible spectacle. It had a huge impact on the sporting world because it came after Tony (Jacklin) had won the Open Championship.

John O'Leary working on the practice range (*c*.1970).

John O'Leary celebrates winning the Carroll's Irish Open (August 1982).

'From an Irish point of view it was even better because Christy O'Connor Snr was playing. He was very helpful to me when I started out on tour. I played a lot with him and we had some great times together.'

Despite his confident start to life on tour, John missed out on selection for the 1973 Ryder Cup at Muirfield, but he was never out of the automatic places for the 1975 team and secured his spot comfortably.

The GB & I team, captained by Bernard Hunt, featured six rookies in total and included two other Irishmen, Eamonn Darcy and, maintaining the family tradition, Christy O'Connor Jnr.

'There's no question about it, making the Ryder Cup team was a huge thing for me. I disagree with this talk from some people claiming that it never really counted,' added John.

'That's nonsense. I remember the party we had when Christy was selected for the team — the excitement of the whole thing. We partied through till dawn. It may

'The players and the PGA did not have the best of relationships at the time. They (the PGA) made things very difficult. My girlfriend and my mother were both supposed to come out to the Ryder Cup, but in the end neither of them did.

'You know, we travelled to America super apex — that's the back of the plane. The clothing we had was unsuitable for the heat and there wasn't enough of it.

'I don't want people saying, "listen to yer man complaining about everything", but that is the way it was. There just wasn't the money available. The whole experience gave me the chance to see for myself the opportunities that were available if we could grasp them.'

To take advantage of those possibilities the players needed to be in control of their own affairs, and John was determined to see the breakaway from the PGA succeed. 'I was totally committed to it. Remember, in those days our opportunities to travel, to play in America, were very limited,' said John.

> ## 'There's no question about it, making the Ryder Cup team was a huge thing for me.'

not have been as competitive as it is today, but it still mattered.'

John's delight at making the team was diluted somewhat by the ongoing problems with the PGA over the proposed split by the tour players. As a leading light in plans to form what became the 'European Tour', John found a number of obstacles placed in his way.

'I have mixed emotions about the whole thing. Nobody will ever understand how we got through it, how we fought for our own independence,' he added.

'When I won the Irish Open (1982) I got into nothing. The Irish Open, along with the PGA Championship, were the two biggest events outside the Open, but it meant nothing.

'Now, if you're in the top 30 you're eligible for this, and if you're in the top 50 you're eligible for that. The opportunities are incredible. With the formation in 1975 of what is now known as the European Tour, we started with a clean sheet of paper and filled it in as we went along. We were trying to make it better for everyone — to put the bricks in place.'

The strained relationship between the players and the PGA could have developed into open hostility, but common sense prevailed, with the players remaining committed to the event and particularly to their captain, Bernard Hunt.

'Bernard was one of the great people of golf over the years and a lovely, lovely man,' added John. 'The captain's role was completely different back then. It bears no resemblance to what a captain does today. Bernard did his best to keep everyone involved and make everyone part of the situation. Personally, I couldn't have wished for more.'

Hunt had captained the side which lost at Muirfield in 1973. Prior to the match he had been confident of victory and had voiced his expectations in the press. This time around, he was far less vocal about his team's chances, and with good reason. GB & I were about to face one of the strongest US sides that has ever been assembled.

The team featured seven US Open winners, three Open winners, two Masters champions and four PGA champions. Jack Nicklaus, Lee Trevino and Tom Weiskopf formed the backbone of the team which was supplemented by three outstanding rookies, Hale Irwin, Bob Murphy and Johnny Miller.

Only two of the team, J. C. Snead and Murphy, had not won a major and the American captain, Arnold Palmer, would have qualified for GB & I after winning the British PGA and the Spanish Open!

By comparison, Hunt was relying on the experience of Tony Jacklin, Brian Barnes and Brian Huggett to drive his team forward and coax performances out of his rookies — Tommy Horton, Eamonn Darcy, Guy Hunt, Norman Wood, Christy O'Connor Jnr and John O'Leary.

Hunt must have known that realistically his team had no chance of victory. The bookies refused to take bets on an outright US victory. That was seen as a foregone conclusion; it was simply a matter of how much they would win by.

'There was no question about it. We felt we were up against it. But we still felt we could give it a good go. We were optimistic,' said John.

Practice went well although heavy rain hampered things for both sides.

'It was a typical American course and the rain left it playing very long, much longer than the stated 7,045 yards. You had to be able to hit long, high iron shots and I was fine with it,' said John.

The conditions clearly hindered the shorter hitters and Tommy Horton voiced his opinion: 'If you're not six feet tall and weigh 200 lbs, you'll pay a heavy penalty if you get in the rough stuff.'

John's time in America had left him better equipped than many of his team mates when it came to dealing with the unfamiliar conditions.

'I was unusual and very privileged in that respect. It's not like today. Because of the structures the tour has in place now, the guys play all over the world,' said John.

'If you take the team as a whole, with the exception of

> ## 'The captain's role was completely different back then. It bears no resemblance to what a captain does today.'

John O'Leary in action during the Open Championship at Muirfield (July 1972).

John O'Leary receives the winner's trophy from Don Carroll at the Carroll's Irish Open (August 1982).

Tony Jacklin, Brian Barnes and myself, it was totally new territory for most of them. Some of them had never even been to America.'

The omens weren't good and the enormity of the task facing GB & I was made apparent when the matches got under way and they lost the opening foursomes 4-0.

John made his debut partnering another rookie, Tommy Horton, in the last match of the morning series against the irrepressible Lee Trevino and J. C. Snead.

'Tommy started off with a lovely drive down the middle and I had an iron in my hand for the second shot but half-shanked/blocked it to the right and that cost us the hole,' said John.

'I lost us the second hole as well with a bad tee shot. It was nerves. Standing on the 1st tee was the most nervous I have ever been. After that everything went out the window. We were always under pressure to catch up.'

opponents completed the outward nine in 32 for a one-hole lead. The next seven holes were halved and the Americans still held their one-hole advantage as they stood on the tee at the 218 yard par three 17th.

Needing a half to keep the match alive, the rookies gave themselves a chance, but they missed the crucial putt and suffered their second 2 and 1 defeat of the day. 'We played better in the fourballs but ultimately still came out on the wrong end of the result,' added John.

It was a similar story for the rest of the team, with Tony Jacklin and Peter Oosterhuis recording the only victory of the day as GB & I suffered a 6½-1½ drubbing.

> ## 'We played better in the fourballs but ultimately still came out on the wrong end of the result.'

Two down after two holes, the rookie pairing could have been swept away, but they clung on and drew level after nine holes before John holed a long putt from off the green at the 11th to surprisingly put GB & I one up.

The Americans responded immediately and levelled things at the 446 yard par four 12th and then Snead holed out with a wonderful bunker shot at the 13th to keep the sides all square. That proved to be the turning point, with the US winning the 14th and 15th before eventually closing the match out 2 and 1.

Despite the shaky start, the O'Leary/Horton pairing impressed Hunt sufficiently to convince him that they deserved another go, this time anchoring the afternoon fourballs. Once again the pair found themselves facing Lee Trevino who had a new partner, Hale Irwin.

Hunt's confidence was repaid by the two rookies as they went to the turn in 33 shots. Unfortunately, their

'Any expectations of victory had disappeared at the end of that first day,' said John. 'It was really a matter of damage limitation from then on.'

John was left out of the morning fourballs on day two as Hunt tried desperately to stop the bleeding. His changes had the desired effect of slowing America's progress towards retaining the cup, with GB & I halving two of the morning matches.

John was back for the afternoon foursomes partnering another Irishman, Christy O'Connor Jnr.

'It was great to get the chance to play with Christy, although we came up against Miller and Weiskopf, possibly the best US pairing,' said John.

'Weiskopf had won the Open in 1973 and Miller was right at his peak. On form alone they'd have been right at the top.'

Christy and Eamonn Darcy had already suffered a defeat at the hands of Tom Weiskopf during the afternoon fourballs on day one. Weiskopf had played superb golf, going to the turn in 30 shots.

This time around he didn't need to repeat that form as John and Christy failed to spark. They carded too many bogies and slipped to a 5 and 3 defeat on another terrible day for GB & I.

With the 16 singles to come, America led 12½-3½ and needed just four points for victory. There was no way back for Hunt's men and America retained the cup midway through the morning singles series on the third and final day. Tom Weiskopf, who won all four of his matches, secured the winning point, beating Guy Hunt 5 and 3.

'I wasn't unhappy with how I played. It was a fantastic thing to be part of. Trevino became a great friend. When he was over here, he used to play with Sam Torrance and myself, teaching us new things he'd learned.

'Tom Weiskopf, Jack Nicklaus — I became friendly with all of them. One of the best memories I have was right at the end, when all of us were in the same locker room sharing a beer together.'

The heavy defeat, 21-11, set off more agonising in the press about the viability of the competition and America's perceived invincibility. John's only consideration was playing himself into contention for the 1977 matches, but somehow it never happened. He never played in another Ryder Cup despite being on tour for a further 15 years.

'There was very little between us. I matched him shot for shot, but he holed a few putts when I didn't.'

John was left out of the morning series but reappeared for the afternoon matches with nothing but pride at stake. That was particularly true for Jack Nicklaus who, after losing to Brian Barnes in the morning, then suffered a second defeat at the hands of the Englishman. John faced another rookie, Hale Irwin, who already had 3½ points to his name and eventually made it 4½ with a 2 and 1 victory.

'There was very little between us. I matched him shot for shot, but he holed a few putts when I didn't,' said John.

'That tended to be a feature of a lot of my matches. I was down early in all of them and then I was always chasing to get back in touch. It was disappointing obviously to come away without anything, but generally speaking my game was quite sound.

'I remember at the time thinking to myself, I'll definitely play in three or four of these. It just didn't happen. I suppose once you make something, to make it again is never quite the same,' he said.

'The urgency is never quite there. Don't misunderstand me. I don't want to come across as if I didn't try. I would love to have played in it again. However, not playing never concerned me in the slightest. I have some friends who came close on many occasions and never made it. I feel sorry for them.'

John's hopes of making future cup teams were hampered by the qualification system which is still conducted today over a one-year period. By some quirk, his best years on tour tended to be the even years.

He finished runner-up in the Irish Open in 1978 and later won it in 1982. Both results would have put him in prime position to make the team, had they come in odd years.

John was a regular on tour up until 1989 when a bad car crash left him with serious back and hip problems. Three operations have failed to return him to full mobility, and his hopes of competing on the Seniors Tour are fading.

He is based at the beautiful Buckinghamshire Golf Club in Denham and pours his energies into coaching Matthew Richardson, who was the European Amateur Boys champion in 2004. He has also been able to focus his attention on the continuing expansion of the European Tour and is proud at how far the tour has come in the 30 years since it was conceived.

'I consider myself very privileged. I played on tour for 20 years and made friends all over the world. What the tour has achieved, through Ken Schofield and under the chairmanship of Neil Coles, is fantastic,' he said.

'I don't like blowing my own trumpet but we have a structure that is the envy of other sports. It's owned by the players and run by and for the players. It has taken almost 30 years, but we now have the control we craved all those years ago, and along with the Ryder Cup we are in a great position to move forward.'

If John has any regrets, it's not that he failed to compete more often in the Ryder Cup, it's simply that he hasn't been able to play with today's generation of Ryder Cup stars.

'I haven't hit a ball for in excess of ten years. I haven't been able to play with Darren Clarke, Paul McGinley and Padraig Harrington,' he said.

'I would love to be able to do that, to get a fourball together, throw a few pounds down and then have a beer together afterwards.'

Chapter 9

Christy O'Connor

Christy O'Connor Jnr celebrates his superb approach shot to the 18th green during his Ryder Cup singles match with Fred Couples (September 1989).

Junior

You could be forgiven for boiling Christy O'Connor Junior's career down to one moment in time, one shot even.

His two-iron approach to the 18th green during his singles match with Fred Couples in the 1989 Ryder Cup is the stuff of golfing legend. It was a career-defining moment.

That shot and Christy's overall performance has come to symbolise all that was good about Tony Jacklin's years as European Ryder Cup captain — how he got the best out of his players and how Europe found a competitive edge. Consequently, you might well expect Christy to describe it as the 'best shot he ever hit', but you'd be wrong. In a career spanning three decades, O'Connor has hit more than one 'great' shot.

'Ithink my best effort came the following year in the Dunhill event at St Andrews,' he said.

'Funnily enough, it was also against Fred Couples. We were playing the 17th and I hit a four-iron over the road-hole bunker and stopped it four feet from the pin. He gave me the putt and then tied a handkerchief on to the end of his club and waved it in the air (in mock surrender). He told me he had never seen the equal of it.'

Throughout his career, Christy's great shots didn't always get the credit they deserved. He spent a lifetime being unfairly compared with his uncle, the legendary Christy O'Connor Snr.

'When I hit a good shot, people would say, that's good but your uncle would have hit a better one — I put up with that for a long time,' he said.

His two-iron shot at the Belfry ensured that he would never have to put up with it again.

● ● ● ●

Unlike many of his contemporaries, Christy grew up with the Ryder Cup. It was in the blood, so to speak.

Christy Snr played in ten consecutive Ryder Cups from 1955 to 1973. Junior remembers listening to news of his uncle's exploits on the radio, and the great sense

America's Fred Couples (*right*) concedes defeat to Europe's Christy O'Connor Jnr on the 18th green at the Belfry (September 1989).

of pride that it brought to the family and the whole village of Knocknacarra where they lived.

'It was a huge thing for us in Galway. Christy Snr making the team every second year — never missing for 20 years. It was incredible,' he said.

Growing up, Christy had a ready-made hero, but he admits that golf wasn't always that important to him.

'I played about at it, as opposed to playing the game,' he said.

'I played very little golf as an amateur. To be honest, I didn't have a lot of time. We all worked very hard at home. We had a shop and a farm. The animals always needed to be looked after and we had to fit our schoolwork around that. But Senior being in the game kept us all focused on golf. He was a big influence.'

In more practical terms, Senior gave Christy's brothers, Sean and Frank, a start in the game by taking them on

'When you have no money and no place to go, you have nothing else to do but practise,' he said. 'So I spent a lot of time practising. My game improved and in one year I became a pretty decent player.'

On his return to Ireland, Junior spent two years at Royal Dublin working for his uncle. During that time Senior worked on Christy's swing, tweaking and developing it. Christy also saw at close quarters the attention to detail that was required to compete at the highest level.

'I left Royal Dublin in 1968 and spent some time with my brother Frank in Holland before I got the professional's post at Carlow,' added Christy.

'My other brother Eugene worked as my assistant and I just practised, practised, practised — sometimes for ten hours a day. At that stage I felt that I could be competitive, so I joined the tour in 1970.'

Christy was 22 years old and had been a full-time professional for just three years when he embarked

'I played very little golf as an amateur. To be honest, I didn't have a lot of time.'

as assistants. He did the same for Christy Jnr in 1966 when, after a disappointing 12 months in South Shields working with professional Kevin Wallace, he returned home with no prospect of a job.

Christy describes that year spent in South Shields as one of the most difficult periods of his life. He was 17 years old, away from home, and earning just £3 a week. He struggled to cope, but ironically his golf game improved rapidly. He had travelled to South Shields as no better than a six handicapper, but he returned to Ireland a much better player.

on his tournament career. His uncle, at 46, was still a 'big player' on the tour and Christy remembers often finishing a round and then heading out on to the course to stand with the fans and watch Senior complete his round.

Junior took time to settle into life on tour. His first significant tournament win was the 1973 Carroll's Match Play in Kilkenny, when he beat Jimmy Kinsella 3 and 2. 'It was a tremendous boost for me,' said Christy.

He finally felt comfortable in the pro ranks, and the following year he took another step in the right direction by winning the Zambian Open — his first win outside Ireland.

The Ryder Cup had never been far from Christy's thoughts throughout those early years. He claims there was never any 'outside' pressure to emulate his uncle and play in the event.

The GB & I team, which included two other Irishmen, Eamonn Darcy and John O'Leary, were simply brushed aside by a powerful American team. Christy had been in America before, but this was his first taste of golf, American style.

'It was a big, big difference to the type of courses we played at home,' he said. 'We were quite lucky; we got to play in the World Open at Pinehurst the week

> 'We felt that we weren't the underdogs any more, and that created more pressure.'

'I just really wanted to play in it. There was never any pressure from Senior. Generally, he would have loved me to make it and I certainly wanted to make it,' he said.

What is certain is that every Ryder Cup year over a 20-year period, Christy Jnr planned to make the team and set out his schedule accordingly.

His uncle made his last Ryder Cup appearance at Muirfield in 1973 and two years later, playing some of the best golf of his career, Junior continued the O'Connor tradition by booking his place on the team for the matches in Laurel Valley, Pennsylvania.

'It meant an awful lot for me to step in, and for the O'Connor family not to miss out a year,' he said.

It proved to be something of a breakthrough year for Christy. He won twice on the European Tour, claiming the Martini International in June and then the Carroll's Irish Open at Woodbrook.

He also regained the Irish Match Play title, and followed that up by winning the Irish Dunlop event. He was in prime form, not that it made much difference when it came to taking on the Americans.

before the Ryder Cup, which helped us get used to the conditions. We were wiped by the Americans in the cup but, although it may be hard to imagine, we did play reasonably well that week.

'GB & I were simply not powerful enough at that stage. Getting the Europeans to come on board was the greatest thing for the Ryder Cup.'

Christy played two matches at Laurel Valley, both in the company of fellow Irish rookies. On day one he partnered Eamonn Darcy in the afternoon fourballs against Tom Weiskopf and Lou Graham.

The Irish pair put up a battling performance in the face of some scintillating golf, particularly from Weiskopf, but eventually slipped to a 3 and 2 defeat.

On the afternoon of day two, with heavy rain making conditions difficult, Christy partnered John O'Leary in the foursomes against the most feared American pairing of Weiskopf and Johnny Miller.

'At that time Miller and Weiskopf were winning everything, and who did we get drawn against? The two of them,' said Christy.

The crowd cheers after Christy O'Connor Jnr (*in centre, hands raised*) **records a vital Ryder Cup singles victory over Fred Couples (September 1989).**

Possibly intimidated by their opponents, John and Christy never got going in the match and lost 5 and 3.

'We were up against it right from the start, and I remember John and I hardly said a word to each other during the front nine,' said Christy. 'We turned for home four down and were playing the 11th, a tight par five, and I missed the green right, putting it in a bunker.

'All of a sudden I hear John behind me say, "Jesus, Christy, there's two acres of green and you go and put it in the bunker!"

'It made a big difference having the other Irish lads in the team. It helped with the nerves, naturally, as it was such a big event for us all. But I think we were even more nervous later on when Europe was in a position to win. We felt that we weren't the underdogs any more, and that created more pressure.'

It was the type of pressure that Christy himself wouldn't have to cope with for a further 14 years. In 1975, when his first Ryder Cup came to a close, he could never have imagined that he would have to wait so long to get back into the team. Yet, between 1975 and 89, Christy O'Connor Jnr was the perennial

Christy O'Connor Jnr is overcome by emotion after his Ryder Cup victory over Fred Couples. He is pictured with wife Ann and European team captain Tony Jacklin (September 1989).

Ryder Cup bridesmaid, missing out by the narrowest of margins.

'I feel that I should have made five teams. Now that would have been incredible, to follow Senior by playing in five events,' said Christy.

'In 1977 I finished in 13th place on the order of merit and captain Brian Huggett put me on stand-by. I don't think Tony Jacklin should have been playing that year. He wasn't playing well.

'I missed out twice more by a few pounds, in 1985 and 1987. It was a horrendous feeling, particularly in 1985. I was in 11th position and had played so well all year.

'I fell out with the captain Tony Jacklin over selection in 1985. I felt I was badly done by. I remember going home from the final qualifying event thinking that I had nothing to worry about, that I had made the team. So I think he made a big mistake by not including me that year.'

'I played with Seve Ballesteros in the Spanish Open the week after the Ryder Cup and he beat me by a couple of shots. He told me that he hadn't realised how well I could play,' said Christy.

'He was part of the reason I was not included in the team. He was a huge voice with Jacklin; he got another Spaniard on the team instead.'

Christy was still featuring strongly on tour when the qualifying period for the 1989 Ryder Cup got under way, but following the disappointments of 1985 and 1987 he wasn't pinning his hopes on making the team. That all changed when he won the Jersey European Open in April, beating Denis Durnian in a play-off.

He then hit a purple patch between the end of May and the middle of June, finishing fourth in the Volvo PGA Championship, third in the Dunhill British Masters and seventh in the NM English Open which was held at the Belfry.

> He was back in the Ryder Cup frame, but as the season wore on he failed to force his way into one of the automatic qualifying slots.

Christy had grounds for feeling aggrieved. He had put in a string of high-quality displays in 1985, which included finishing third at the Open at Royal St George's.

Jacklin, in his second term in charge of the team, had persuaded the PGA to change their selection procedure, giving him the chance to make three wildcard choices. He ignored Christy's genuine claims for a place and plumped instead for Nick Faldo, Ken Brown and José Rivero.

He was back in the Ryder Cup frame, but as the season wore on he failed to force his way into one of the automatic qualifying slots and it became clear that he would have to rely once again on a wildcard selection from captain Tony Jacklin.

'I was playing the final qualifying event in Germany and put together two excellent closing rounds (68 and 67),' said Christy. 'My wife Ann was convinced I was going to make the team, but I wasn't so sure. I was never tipped off that I was in line for a captain's pick, although I did get a wee nod from Bernhard Langer in the locker room after finishing the event, but I didn't cop on to it.'

Christy certainly wasn't one of Jacklin's first choices for a wildcard spot, but when Sandy Lyle, based on the US tour, ruled himself out of the event, the captain turned to Christy.

Putting aside any remaining frustration he may have felt following previous selection disappointments, Christy readily accepted the invitation to join the team and committed himself to the European cause.

'It was all forgotten. You had to; there was a job to do,' he said. 'I knew Jacklin before he took over the captaincy and I knew his first wife Vivienne, who was from Northern Ireland. [Vivienne Jacklin died from a brain haemorrhage in 1988.] You have to let things go.'

Christy was 41 when he returned to the Ryder Cup and he found it a completely different animal from the one he had left behind in 1975.

'When I think back on it, in the early days we played to get the lovely bags and stuff, the tickets etc. When I returned, you could sense that the pressure was so much greater, that there was more at stake. The Ryder Cup had grown to be a monster,' he said.

The hype, the press coverage and the fans all caught Christy slightly unawares.

'I'd played in a lot of big tournaments between 1975 and 89,' said Christy. 'I'd played in the old World Cup and nearly won the Open Championship. I had been in the thick of things, but the Ryder Cup is something else.

'The pressure is horrendous. You don't want to let your fans down and you don't want to let your family down. I would have hated myself for not being on the team. But I hated myself when I was on it.'

The Americans, despite having lost the two previous encounters, were installed as favourites to regain the trophy. US Open champion Curtis Strange, Open champion Mark Calcavecchia and USPGA champion

Christy O'Connor Jnr celebrates victory in the Carroll's Irish Open (August 1975).

Christy O'Connor Jnr *(back row, third from left)* **pictured with the rest of the European Ryder Cup team including Ronan Rafferty** *(back row, extreme right)* **(September 1989).**

Payne Stewart led the team. Just for good measure, captain Raymond Floyd went for experience and selected Tom Watson and Lanny Wadkins as his two picks.

Jacklin had a more experienced line-up, backboned by Ballesteros, Langer, Woosnam and Faldo. His one rookie was Warrenpoint-born Ronan Rafferty, the No. 1 golfer on the European Tour at the time.

Christy sat out proceedings on day one as Europe fought back from a poor opening foursomes series to sweep the fourballs and take a 5-3 lead.

Jacklin gave the Galway man his chance during the morning foursomes on day two, partnering Ronan Rafferty against Mark Calcavecchia and Ken Green. It was a selection decision that baffled Christy, who had spent the week practising with José Maria Canizares.

'I think it was probably a bad pairing. We were a nervous pairing. Both of us should have been with a more experienced man,' said Christy.

'I knew Canizares very well; our games suited each other. He looked round at me when Jacklin announced the pairings. He couldn't believe it.'

'The pressure is horrendous. You don't want to let your fans down and you don't want to let your family down.'

Christy O'Connor Jnr celebrates victory in the British Senior Open Championship at Royal Portrush (July 1999).

The two Irishmen never managed to gel and with both of them struggling on the greens, they turned for home three down. The situation got worse after the turn and with six holes left, they found themselves five down.

With defeat seemingly imminent, they relaxed and played some of their best golf, winning the 13th and 15th to trail by three with three to play before the Americans managed to close things out on the 16th for a 3 and 2 victory.

Christy still hadn't a Ryder Cup point to his name, but as a team the Europeans had weathered a US fight back, and going into the final day singles the two-point lead was still intact at 9-7.

Unfortunately, Christy's nervy display in the foursomes did little to alter the perception within some sections of the media that Jacklin had made a mistake by including him. Members of the press who had queried the decision in the first place now wrote him off.

'I knew what the press were writing about me, but I was determined to do well at the Belfry,' said Christy. 'On the morning of the singles, Ann and I decided we weren't going to read any papers. We went downstairs into the breakfast room and there must have been 50 papers scattered around the place and the one that caught my eye had a big headline along the lines of "O'Connor weak link in European team".

'I still remember seeing it, it was such a terrible downer. Both Ann and Christy Senior reminded me that I had played well all year and all I had to do was go out and give it 100 per cent.

'I was playing against Fred Couples, the No. 1 golfer in the world at the time and the longest hitter at that time. I knew he was going to be much, much longer off the tee than me, but I was prepared for that.'

Christy's caddie, Matthew Byrne, remembers how fired up the Galway man was when he met up with him on the practice range ahead of his clash with Couples. Spurred on by some words of encouragement from Seve Ballesteros, Christy got off to a great start by nailing a 20 foot putt at the 1st to go one up on Couples and set the tone for the match.

He refused to be intimidated by the American and he felt that if he could stay in touch, he had a chance of victory over the closing holes. Couples edged ahead at the 5th, but a long putt from Christy at the 9th brought the two men level again.

The American won the 10th with a birdie, but there was still only one in it as they reached the 16th. From the middle of the fairway, Christy hit an immaculate wedge which finished three feet from the hole. With Couples two-putting for par, Christy looked over his birdie putt and somehow managed to sneak it in the side door to level the match once again.

The 17th was halved in par, with Christy hitting a fantastic two-iron which ran through the back of the green, to take the match down the 18th.

Europe had battled back into contention after a shaky start to the singles, but with the early defeats of Ballesteros and Langer, Christy's match had taken on extra significance. Victory for the Galway man would leave Europe requiring one and a half points from

'I was playing against Fred Couples, the No. 1 golfer in the world at the time and the longest hitter at that time.'

the final five matches to win the trophy for the third consecutive time.

Christy hit a decent drive off the 18th before Couples replied with a huge effort that finished a full 90 yards ahead of the Irishman.

Jacklin offered Christy some advice as he considered his approach to the green. 'If you get this on the green, you'll win the hole,' he said.

Christy reached his ball and was happy to see it sitting up on the tightly cut fairway. 'I had over 200 yards to the green and knew my two-iron was the right club for the job,' said Christy. 'Jacklin came over. "One more swing for Ireland," he said. I made a perfect execution. I caught it 110 per cent.'

With the crowd going wild, Christy's approach flew straight at the flag, pitched on the bottom of the green and rolled up to within three feet.

way of the Americans and the event finished with the sides level at 14 apiece.

Tony Adamson was standing beside the 18th green when Christy fired that wonderful approach shot into the green. A native of Donegal, Adamson was the voice of BBC Radio golf for 20 years up until his retirement in 2004. Of all the Irish performances he has commentated on, Christy's display at the Belfry sticks in his mind.

'Of all the Irish players who contributed to European success over the last 20 years, Christy O'Connor's will live in my memory for a hell of a long time,' he said.

'That two-iron that he played — I think that will live longer in the memory of Irish golfing fans than many. Christy O'Connor Snr would have been proud of it. I think it was the most famous two-iron ever hit in Ireland's history from my point of view.

'It was 240 yards, something like it, and he hit it to 3½ feet! Couples was gobsmacked, and he shanked his

> ## With the crowd going wild, Christy's approach flew straight at the flag, pitched on the bottom of the green and rolled up to within three feet.

'It clearly rattled Couples,' said Christy. The American, with only a short iron in his hands, shanked his approach into a greenside bunker, and from there he failed to get down in two.

He conceded Christy's putt and with the Belfry going crazy, the Galway man offered a silent prayer before being engulfed by his wife and team mates. Christy's fantastic win was soon followed by another from his good friend José Maria Canizares. Europe had retained the trophy, but the remaining four matches went the

approach. It absolutely destroyed Couples. The noise when Christy came on the green was just unbelievable. It will live long with me and of course he burst into tears and his wife was there on the green with him.

'I remember him saying to me that Tony Jacklin had said to him as he was approaching his second shot, if you could put Couples under pressure, I think you'll win the hole and the match and just have a good swing. He just hit it. It was an extraordinary moment, a great moment for Irish golf.'

Europe's Christy O'Connor Jnr acknowledges the fans after his Ryder Cup singles victory over Fred Couples (September 1989).

Chapter 10

Eamonn Darcy

Eamonn Darcy in action at the Murphy's Irish Open at Druids Glen (July 1999).

It takes a lot to get Eamonn Darcy angry.

Throughout a long, profitable and highly competitive career he has managed to maintain a sense of perspective. Golf is his living, but it is still a game.

The only time Eamonn ever got genuinely angry on a golf course was during his famous singles victory over Ben Crenshaw in the 1987 Ryder Cup at Muirfield Village. It wasn't enough that he had let a three-hole lead slip; the Delgany man was also battling with the crowd.

Eamonn Darcy celebrates his Ryder Cup singles victory over Ben Crenshaw at Muirfield Village, Ohio, USA (September 1987).

'I was playing the short par four 14th and hit a terrible second shot way left into the crowd. It was stone dead,' said Eamonn.

'When we got up to the ball there was some confusion about the ball having been kicked back towards the green, so we had to get a referee and eventually it was established that the ball had run down the bank.'

He was left with a very difficult pitch and knew he was going to struggle to keep it on the green.

'As I stood over the ball someone in the crowd behind me said, "miss it." I hit a great pitch. It just trickled off the edge of the green and I then failed to hole my 15 foot putt for a half,' said Eamonn.

If Europe were to win the Ryder Cup in America for the first time, it was going to come down to the last few singles matches. He needed to get half a point at the very least.

After a bad tee shot at the 15th he somehow managed to get on to the green in three and eventually made a tricky ten-footer for a half. It was only a short respite because Crenshaw then hit a superb long iron into the par three 16th which almost finished in the hole. Eamonn failed to find the putting surface and his bogey left him trailing for the first time.

'My match was becoming really critical at this stage. Ken Brown was getting hammered behind me, but Seve looked like he was doing well,' said Eamonn.

> 'When we got up to the ball there was some confusion about the ball having been kicked back towards the green.'

'I walked off the green and said to Ben, "You and I could be having a nice game if it wasn't for these arseholes." You know, as we walked on to the 1st green that day there was a big fat guy in the gallery. He was frothing at the mouth and screaming, "Kill him Ben, kill him. No prisoners today." I thought to myself, here we go — it was going to be that kind of day.'

• • • •

Back on the 15th tee, Eamonn was trying desperately to stay in the present. He was frustrated with himself for letting Crenshaw back into the match and he was fuming with the idiot in the crowd who had tried to put him off.

He was also becoming aware of just how important his match was going to be. Ahead of him the likes of Lyle, Faldo and Woosnam were all behind in their matches.

With the pressure at its greatest, it was the American who cracked first. Crenshaw, who had putted with a variety of clubs after breaking his putter on the 6th, pushed his drive down the 17th and was forced to hit a blind second shot which got caught up in a bunker.

'I wasn't aware that Ben had broken his putter,' said Eamonn. 'I thought he was putting with his one-iron because the greens were so quick and he had missed a couple on the front nine.'

As the American faltered, Eamonn seized the opportunity and hit a superb iron into the 17th which finished no more than four feet from the hole. Crenshaw failed to extricate himself from the greenside bunker and conceded the hole to level the match.

'Even as I walked off the 17th green and looked at the scoreboard, I thought we were going to lose,' said Eamonn.

'Personally I was buoyant. I had won the 17th and I remember walking on to the 18th tee thinking to myself that this guy is feeling the pressure as much as me. I was determined to try and stay in the present. It was the classic case of one shot at a time. You know, the Ryder Cup is so big, that if your mind wanders at all you can get swamped.'

With all to play for, Eamonn fired a solid three-wood down the fairway. Crenshaw, clearly rattled, tweaked his drive into the stream that ran down the left-hand side of the fairway.

Forced to take a penalty drop, he proceeded to hit his third shot into one of the bunkers at the front of the green. With the match at his mercy, Eamonn's three-iron approach caught the top of the bunker and fell back in — Crenshaw still had a chance.

'I was unlucky with my second shot. It was right on top of the flag, but it was just too low,' added Eamonn.

'I was hoping he'd miss his. It was by far the easier of the two putts,' said Eamonn.

'If I missed mine, it was likely to finish 20 feet away. But I was confident enough that I would hole it. I wasn't thinking about missing.'

With the outcome of the Ryder Cup now hinging on his putt, Eamonn somehow coaxed the ball down the hill and into the cup.

'In hindsight, the way it all happened was a fairytale. We all get a chance somewhere,' he said.

'Match play is a strange thing. You can play well and get beaten and play badly and win. I was playing solidly during the 1987 Ryder Cup. I made a number of silly mistakes on the back nine to let Ben back into the match, but I was playing solidly. You know, I think that I was just ready at that stage of my career to hole that putt.'

> With the outcome of the Ryder Cup now hinging on his putt, Eamonn somehow coaxed the ball down the hill and into the cup.

'It hit the top of the bunker and came back. When I got up to it, I could see it was in an awkward spot. It was right underneath the lip. I had no choice but to make sure I got out. That's why I had to hit it so hard and that's why it went past the hole.'

Both men found the green from the bunker, but Crenshaw was left with the easier uphill putt. Still putting with his one-iron, the Texan holed his putt for a five and the pressure switched once again to the Irishman who was looking over a slippery, downhill four-footer to win.

Victory had been a long time coming for Eamonn — 12 years and four Ryder Cups to be exact.

'It was great to play a significant part in winning the trophy,' he said. 'Even though we all claim the Ryder Cup is a team event, it's nice that having had a reasonably successful career, I was able to put my stamp on the event. For the putts I'd missed and the matches I'd lost, I'd given my all in that match, which was a big contributing factor to winning for the first time in America.'

US Ryder Cup team captain Jack Nicklaus congratulates Eamonn Darcy after the Irishman defeated Ben Crenshaw (September 1987).

The European Ryder Cup team celebrates success at Muirfield Village. Eamonn Darcy is pictured extreme right. (September 1987).

Eamonn's career is now stretching into its 37th season. He has been a professional golfer since he was 16 years old. For 25 of those, he was one of the most competitive golfers on the European Tour and he did so with a twirling, idiosyncratic swing that shocked the purists and amazed the fans.

In many respects, Eamonn's unique action has helped him stand out from the crowd. Peering down a fairway you may not be able to see who is about to play, but once you see the club moving you know it's Eamonn Darcy.

His swing is a product of a hurling background and although he was tempted on a number of occasions to make major changes, he has remained true to it. There was a certain stubbornness there, a determination to do it 'his way', but early on in his career he understood that it's not how it looks that matters, but how many.

'Looking back, it might have been a mistake that I didn't change my swing, but I started to make a few bob early, mainly as a result of my very good short game,' he said.

'I knew how my swing worked and I was told that to change it would involve taking two or three years off and not competing. I couldn't afford to do that. People saw all the whirling about, but they didn't know the game.'

Growing up, Eamonn never had any thoughts about being a golfer, even though his family had close ties with the game.

'My great granduncle, Pat Doyle, was a professional in Florida. He was the first professional at Delgany back in the early 1900s,' said Eamonn.

'Jimmy Martin (former tour player and Ryder Cup player) was a cousin of mine, my uncle Jack was a professional in Bristol and my brother Martin is the professional at Knockanally. My dad, who introduced me to the game, was a very good player. He was a scratch man at Delgany.'

Eamonn caddied for his father on the odd occasion, but he had no love for the game. His first love was horses

'I remember my first competition. I played at Delgany in a Leinster Alliance as a 16-year-old assistant,' said Eamonn.

'There was a bit of money to be made in those days if you were capable of being competitive. After the round I walked back across the course to our house, which backed on to the 4th green.

> ## 'I remember my first competition. I played at Delgany in a Leinster Alliance as a 16-year-old assistant.'

and he dreamed of being a jockey. Unfortunately, he simply grew too big. With the horse riding avenue closed to him, he had to look elsewhere for a career.

'Harry Bradshaw's brother, Jimmy, was talking to Wattie Sullivan one day (Walter Sullivan was the professional at the Grange GC),' said Eamonn. 'Wattie was looking for a young fella to help him out at the club, and Jimmy told him that he knew just the person — me. That's how I started. I went to the Grange and did my apprenticeship there, three years with Wattie.'

By Eamonn's own admission, he was no better than a 12 handicap when he joined the professional ranks. He had never played golf regularly, had never taken it seriously.

'The boys talked me into it. They encouraged me. I was good with people, and the idea was that I would become a club professional and make a comfortable living,' he said.

Winning tournaments, making money, playing in the Ryder Cup were the furthest things from Eamonn's mind when he embarked on his new career. He wasn't even a particularly good club golfer.

'My dad was waiting for me and he asked me how things had gone. I told him I'd had a bad day on the greens. "That's a pity," he said. "What did you score?"

'86,' I said.

'"Well," he says, "I'll tell you what I would do now if I was you. There's a big shovel in the shed and I would go out there, dig a big hole and then jump into it and I'd stay there for a few days."

'He got a real shock when I made the Ryder Cup team seven years later.'

Eamonn spent three years with Wattie, three years during which just being around golf every day helped to bring down his handicap. He then moved to Erewash Valley GC in Derbyshire as assistant to David Parsonage where he stayed for almost ten years.

It was a move designed to give him the opportunity to play more competitive golf. He made the best of the facilities on offer, particularly the chipping green near the shop, on which he would while away the hours between serving customers.

He insists that those early years were essential in his development, but it was his forays on to the Zambian Tour during the 1970s that convinced him he could make a decent living at the game.

'It was fantastic competition out there. We went out at the beginning of March for about five or six weeks. All the boys flew down there because it was simply the only place to get playing any sort of golf,' he said.

'I suppose, when you compare it to today and events all over the world, it just shows you how much the tour has changed. I went down with all the other Irish guys, the likes of Christy Jnr, Mick Murphy, David Jones, Jimmy Kinsella and Christy Snr. It was a fantastic way to learn how to compete. I also started making a few bob, winning the odd week.'

'There was no team spirit. There were no meetings, no get togethers,' he said.

'I was a little overawed. It was my first time in America playing among the American public. It was tough being so young.'

Thankfully, Eamonn was able to rely on the help and support of the two other Irish rookies on the team, John O'Leary and Christy O'Connor Jnr. The three Irishmen made sure they enjoyed the whole experience, but they had little success on the course.

Eamonn and Christy, close friends and regular playing partners, made their debuts together in the afternoon fourballs on day one. The two rookies competed well but were eventually beaten 3 and 2.

> 'I was a little overawed. It was my first time in America playing among the American public. It was tough being so young.'

His confidence and his self-belief grew. By the time he was making his Ryder Cup debut at Laurel Valley, Pennsylvania, in 1975, Eamonn was one of the most consistent players on tour and had developed a bit of a swagger.

'I wasn't really surprised to make the team. I just took it in my stride,' he said. He was 23 years old, at that stage the youngest ever to play in the event, but he hadn't a clue what he was getting himself into.

The Ryder Cup had barely entered his consciousness growing up. American dominance was such that the event looked to be on its last legs. The GB & I players had grown used to getting beaten, and that mood left a lasting impression on the young Irishman.

On day two, team captain Bernard Hunt paired Darcy with the more experienced Guy Hunt, and the two men combined to secure half a point from their game with Al Geiberger and Raymond Floyd. One down after 17, Darcy played the last superbly, firing a four-wood into the green from 220 yards and then rolling in the 15 foot putt to tie the match.

Hunt clearly felt the pairing had merit and put them out again in the afternoon foursomes against Geiberger and Floyd. Unfortunately, the magic had worn off and a terrible front nine left the GB & I pair with too much to do over the closing holes on their way to a 3 and 2 defeat.

The final day saw Eamonn drawn against one of the US team's elder statesmen, 37-year-old Billy Casper, in

The victorious European team pose for a picture on their return from Muirfield Village. Eamonn Darcy is pictured back row, extreme left (September 1987).

the singles. The two-time US Open champion, playing in his final Ryder Cup, was never really threatened and coasted to a 3 and 2 victory.

Eamonn finished the event with only half a point to his name, but he was one of the few GB & I players who returned home with their reputations enhanced following a 21-11 hammering. Two years later, at Royal Lytham and St Anne's, Eamonn was again in the thick of the action, but this time he was no longer a rookie.

'We were playing on a links course, we had the home crowd and I enjoyed it,' said Eamonn. 'I had more control of my game. I was not a little kid any longer; I was seasoned. I felt I could carry my own weight.'

As a measure of Eamonn's growing stature in the game, he was paired with Tony Jacklin in the opening series of foursomes on day one. Jacklin was something of a spent force by 1977, but he was clearly the only world-class performer on the GB & I team.

They faced Ed Sneed and Don January and should really have come away with a full point. Two up with four to play, they failed to close the Americans out, and Sneed almost snatched victory with a putt on the last.

Eamonn and Jacklin were paired together again for the day two fourballs against Dave Hill and Dave Stockton. After nine holes the sides were level, but only because Eamonn holed a couple of outrageously long putts.

Jacklin was playing terrible golf and Eamonn simply couldn't carry the fight by himself. From the turn the

Eamonn Darcy pictured following his victory in the Dubai Desert Classic (February 1990).

Americans won five of the next six holes to claim a 5 and 3 victory.

Stockton later declared: 'Jacklin was playing so poorly that we thought we were playing only Eamonn Darcy.'

Jacklin's form was so bad that GB & I captain Brian Hugget made the decision to drop him for the final day singles. Jacklin was incensed by the decision and Eamonn remembers the row it caused but claims it had little effect on team morale — there wasn't much of a 'team' to begin with.

GB & I were trailing 7½-5½ as the singles began. It was going to take a miracle for them to turn things around,

and despite a gutsy display they never managed it, splitting the ten singles 5-5.

Eamonn took on US Open champion Hubert Green in the singles, but once again came out on the wrong side of the result.

'I remember playing my heart out in the singles, but I got beaten on the last. I played like hell in that match. Someone told me afterwards that I would have won seven or eight of the other matches,' said Eamonn.

'Green played very well that day. I think the scores were something like 66-67; that can happen in match play.'

The hard facts of the matter were that from seven Ryder Cup games, Eamonn had gathered just two half points. However, his enthusiasm for the event still remained.

'I was still interested in playing in the Ryder Cup,' he said. 'You wanted to play on the team. You always felt that you should be on it because it meant you were playing half decent.'

At least, that was the idea. When Eamonn next found himself on the European team (as it had become then) in 1981 at Walton Heath, his game was at a low ebb. He finished ninth on the order of merit that year, but by his own admission he was playing badly. The state of his game was reflected in the fact that he made just one appearance before the singles.

alone wasn't going to be enough against Nicklaus.

'My game was simply not in good shape at that time,' said Eamonn. 'I played terrible against Nicklaus. I gave him the first two holes. It was a bad Ryder Cup for me.'

Nicklaus brought his Ryder Cup career to an end with a 5 and 3 win as the Americans won 18½-9½, their biggest victory away from home.

By the time Eamonn forced his way back on to the team in 1987, the Ryder Cup had changed beyond recognition. Europe, under Jacklin, was now a force to be reckoned with, and when the team travelled to Muifield, Jacklin made it clear his intention was to win.

'By the time Eamonn forced his way back on to the team in 1987, the Ryder Cup had changed beyond recognition.'

Captain John Jacobs paired him with Bernard Gallacher in the afternoon fourballs on day one against Hale Irwin and Raymond Floyd. With Gallacher now playing the role Eamonn had once filled with Jacklin, the sides were level at the turn.

The Americans edged ahead over the next couple of holes before Gallacher holed a monster eagle putt on the 14th to level the match again. With Eamonn almost reduced to the role of bystander, Gallacher and Floyd scrapped it out over the closing holes, with Floyd coming out on top courtesy of birdie putts on the 16th and 17th for a 2 and 1 victory.

Eamonn wasn't seen again until the final match of the singles series on day three. Out of form and low on confidence, he ended up drawn against Jack Nicklaus. Jacobs tried to talk the encounter up, claiming that he knew how much courage Eamonn had. But courage

Eamonn found himself playing in a real 'team' and he thrived in it.

'There was a different buzz with Jacklin as captain,' he said. 'Everything was first class. We went over with one aim, to win. Jacklin made it clear that it was a team thing.

'He explained that if people were not playing well they would not start. If the guys were getting points on the board, he was going to keep them out there. That was his way and I was fine with it. I got on well with him. He spoke plainly and he was totally in touch with the players. He had been there and done it. You could relate to him.'

Eamonn was 35 when he holed that winning putt against Crenshaw. It had taken him a long time to get there, but for the first time in his Ryder Cup career he had been part of a real 'team' and his game had responded in that environment. The experience left him eager for more, and he was bitterly disappointed not to be in the frame for the return to the Belfry in 1989.

Two years later, and with one qualifying event left, Eamonn looked a nailed-on certainty to make the team for the matches at Kiawah Island.

'I was probably playing the best golf of my career at that stage,' he said. 'I had taken the experience from Muirfield into the following years. Anytime I got into a tight situation, I would refer back to the Ryder Cup and tell myself that it was not pressure compared to Muirfield.'

make the team you'll not get picked", I'd have gone to Germany. I really had a point in me in Kiawah.'

Gallacher has always maintained that he has no recollection of that conversation with Eamonn, but the whole episode certainly took some gloss off Eamonn's Ryder Cup experiences.

'I was disappointed by the whole thing. I was hard done by,' said Eamonn. 'Had I even gone to Germany and just teed it up in the event, I'd have made the team.

'It's amazing how it turned out. David Gilford finished around £50 ahead of me. Philip Walton told me he

> 'I was probably playing the best golf of my career at that stage. I had taken the experience from Muirfield into the following years.'

The rights and wrongs of how Eamonn eventually missed out on the trip to Kiawah will probably never be fully understood, but he still feels a great sense of injustice about it.

'Bernard Gallacher (1991 captain) was in my house. He was borrowing a set of golf clubs and we were talking about the Ryder Cup,' said Eamonn. 'I told him I wasn't going to play in Germany (the final qualifying event). He told me that it wasn't a problem, that I was on the team.

'So we go on to discuss who he is likely to pick and we talk about Mark James's chances. He told me he wouldn't pick him unless he finished inside the top 20.

'To cut a long story short, three people went past me in Germany and he picked Mark, who finished 27th in the money list. If he had said to me, "Eamonn, if you don't

was playing the 17th and somebody stole his ball. He took a seven. If he had made six, I would have been in the team. The week of the German Open, the German mark got stronger and there was more money to be won at the tournament.'

While Eamonn enjoyed a family holiday, three men, Sam Torrance, David Gilford and Paul Broadhurst, all passed him on the money list. Eamonn slipped from seventh to tenth and missed out.

It was a cruel end to Eamonn's Ryder Cup career, particularly for someone who had shown great loyalty to the European Tour over the years.

'Maybe it was destiny,' he said. 'I couldn't improve on what I did in 1987.'

Eamonn Darcy at the Open Championship in Troon (July 1982).

Chapter 11

Des Smyth

Des Smyth watches his drive from the 10th tee, third round, Smurfit Irish PGA Championship at Castlerock Golf Club, Co. Derry (October 2001).

In hindsight, Des Smyth should probably have grabbed Ken Brown by the arm, took him to one side and asked him what the hell he was playing at.

Here he was, making his debut in the Ryder Cup against Hale Irwin and Tom Kite and his more experienced partner was refusing to speak to him!

'I was very nervous starting out, which wasn't helped by the fact that I knew we were up against a great pairing,' said Des.

'Ken reacted very badly. He didn't want to play with me; he only wanted to play with Mark (James). He looked like he didn't have any interest at all. It was very, very awkward.'

Des Smyth plays from the rough during the Ryder Cup at Walton Heath (September 1981).

It was certainly not the start the Drogheda man had dreamed of. As a wildcard choice, Des felt he had to validate his selection by performing well, but there was little chance of that with Brown throwing what Des later described as a 'wobbly'.

'We played that year (1979) at the Greenbrier in West Virginia, and it was a new thing for me. I was under a lot of pressure to perform,' he said.

'At the start of the year I hadn't been thinking about the Ryder Cup and there had been no indication the year before that I would make the team. I moved almost from obscurity into the higher echelons of the game.'

The Americans didn't really have to do that much as the European pairing reeled off a succession of bogeys on their way to an embarrassing 7 and 6 defeat.

'The fact of the matter is that they seemed to give us the match early on,' said Irwin.

'The heart did not seem to be in the body. We were grateful recipients of their bad play. Ken hit some just terrible shots. Des hit some good ones, but when he did Ken promptly put him in jail somewhere.

'Foursomes is an unusual sort of game. You have to be able to communicate with your partner. It was obvious

> ## 'At the start of the year I hadn't been thinking about the Ryder Cup and there had been no indication the year before that I would make the team.'

Now, in the full glare of the Ryder Cup, Des found himself in something of a nightmare.

Mark James came into the event carrying an injury and had played with Brown in the morning fourballs, losing to Lee Trevino and Fuzzy Zoeller. Severely hampered by the injury, James received an injection during lunch but was unable to return to action in the afternoon, and at the last minute Des was drafted in to partner Brown in the foursomes.

'It was not a great introduction to the Ryder Cup,' said Des. 'He (Brown) didn't make a big effort. I realised early on that I had a problem so I just tried to get on with my own game, but Kite and Irwin, both world-class players, saw that we were having problems and exploited it.'

there was no rapport between them. There was not even the slightest bit of idle conversation. Smyth didn't play well, and Brown played like he didn't care.'

In the aftermath of a performance which celebrated golf journalist, Peter Dobereiner, described as 'nothing less than a disgrace', European captain John Jacobs publicly voiced his support for Brown. 'Ken Brown did nothing wrong, but he did fail to communicate,' said Jacobs.

Privately, Jacobs acknowledged he had made a mistake and apologised to Des for throwing him into the deep end.

'Afterwards when we chatted about it, he said, "I should have put you and Michael King in together,"' said Des.

'I had played my practice rounds with Michael. We practised together for two or three days and were getting on well.

'When Mark got injured, John should have put a whole new team in. That's why it's so important for a Ryder Cup captain to know which players get on well together, and to understand which pairings will gel when the pressure is on.'

●   ●   ●   ●

You can be certain that Des Smyth will be doing everything in his power to ensure Europe gets the pairings right when the Ryder Cup gets under way at the K Club.

As one of Ian Woosnam's vice-captains he will have a direct input into the decision-making process, and you can guarantee he will be taking it very seriously.

Woosnam and Smyth are old friends from their early years on tour together in the mid-1970s, and it came as no surprise to anyone when the Welshman named Smyth as part of his backroom team in June 2005. Woosnam had promised there would be an Irish element to the captaincy, and the close relationship between the two men made Smyth an obvious front runner.

'I felt that was the right way for team spirit as well as the crowd (to have an Irishman involved),' said Woosnam. 'I have known Des since I first came on tour in 1976. We shared a room together in Kenya when I was a very young lad and, you know, we've been close ever since.

'Des is going to be a very special part of my team. He's a very popular figure in Ireland and everywhere he has played.'

Des's appointment received unanimous approval from two of Ireland's recent Ryder Cup stars, Paul McGinley and Padraig Harrington.

'There's a huge amount of respect for Des on tour,' said Paul. 'He is such a level-headed individual and has so much experience, he will bring a lot to the table when it comes to decision-making and player pairings.'

Harrington was also positive about the impact Des would have on the event. 'Des is a real gentleman and you can always rely on him to say the right thing, which is very important in the Ryder Cup,' said Padraig. 'He will also keep team spirits up. Because he has played himself, Des will know when to give someone a kick up the backside and when to put an arm around someone else.'

Des was thrilled to be asked and jumped at the opportunity to play a role at the K Club.

'Ian spoke to me shortly after he was appointed to say he had me in mind, but asked me to keep it under wraps,' said Des. 'I was hoping for it, of course, but you don't count your chickens. I'm delighted to be invited on board. I'm very excited to be part of the Ryder Cup in Ireland.'

While conceding that the Ryder Cup, as an event, has grown considerably since he last played in 1981, Des feels that some things have always remained constant.

'The Ryder Cup was always a big deal. What has changed is the media interest and the television coverage.'

'The Ryder Cup was always a big deal. What has changed is the media interest and the television coverage. It will be a nervous time at the K Club, but it will never be as nerve-racking as when you are a player,' he said.

What has definitely changed in that period is that Europe is now seen as a viable, consistent opponent to the Americans. Des will be involved with a team which, going by recent results, should be considered favourites to retain the Ryder Cup. That wasn't always the case.

When Des made his Ryder Cup debut in the very first European team back in 1979, there were still a lot of question marks over the inclusion of European players.

'Whether this team will play with the same fire under the European banner as the Ryder Cup teams did, I take leave to doubt, just as I doubt whether the public interest (and with it the public income) will be as intense', wrote Peter Dobereiner.

Des Smyth celebrates Ryder Cup foursomes victory over Hale Irwin and Ray Floyd at Walton Heath (September 1981).

Des Smyth plays from a bunker during the Open Championship at Muirfield, Scotland (July 2002).

However Des, like many of his fellow professionals, embraced the inclusion of European players, and he remains committed to the European cause.

'We're much stronger now as part of a European team,' he said. 'The Americans were losing interest in it (Ryder Cup). The early European teams were still beaten by big margins, but we knew we were getting stronger.

'The players knew the gap was starting to close and that standards were improving. A lot of talented young players were forcing their way on to the team, and we managed to take the odd point off some of those great American players. We knew we could do better, as has been proved since.

'We're all part of Europe now. If there were 12 continental players on the team I'd still be supporting them, feeling it was my team. There wouldn't have to

America,' said Des.

'I didn't have much experience of playing in the States. It was a bit of a new deal for me, but I enjoyed it immensely. It was a wonderful place and a great golf course.

'It was a completely different environment for me and it took me a while to get used to playing in America. The young players today don't have that problem. They travel so much more than we did in those days. The only time players from here went to America was by getting on a Ryder Cup team. The tour was so small back then. You played in Africa, you played a few events in Europe, but mainly you played your golf in GB & I.'

Des was selected for the 1979 team as one of two wildcards, with Peter Oosterhuis getting the other spot. It came out of the blue and Des describes it as 'the

'I beat Nick Price in the final, which was a bit of a feather in my cap.'

be an Irishman on it, although of course I would love to see as many Irishmen as possible playing.'

Des insists that aside from Ken Brown and Mark James who, in his words 'misbehaved', the first European team which included the two Spaniards Seve Ballesteros and Antonio Garrido came together remarkably well at the Greenbrier in 1979. It may well have been a bit strange for those team members who had previously played on GB & I teams, but Des maintains that, on the whole, the team captained by John Jacobs enjoyed themselves.

'It was not a great experience on the golf course, but everything else I enjoyed. The team camaraderie was very good, and I have some very good memories, particularly as it was one of my earliest excursions to

thrill of a lifetime'. He did feel he was in with a shout after completing his best season on tour, but he never received any indications that he was in the running for selection.

After turning professional in 1974, Des made little impact until 1979 when he claimed his first Irish PGA title (he would go on to win it five more times) and then followed that up with his breakthrough win on tour, the Sun Alliance European Match Play.

'I beat Nick Price in the final, which was a bit of a feather in my cap,' said Des. 'I was playing well and I continued to play well after my win, eventually finishing just outside the top ten on the order of merit. I felt then that I had an outside chance of making the team.'

When the cup committee sat down to choose the two wildcards to represent Europe, they couldn't really ignore the claims of Europe's match play champion. Des's victory over Price earned him a reputation as something of a match play expert, a tag which he has carried throughout his career.

'You can definitely have specialist match play players,' said Des. 'When you are looking at a guy, man to man, eyeball to eyeball, you sometimes play to a higher standard than normal.

'When I was growing up in Bettystown (south of Drogheda) we all played tennis, football and golf. There wasn't that much else to do. I lived less than half a mile away from the Laytown and Bettystown Golf Club, and I was playing golf from around the age of 6. I fell in love with the game and knew in my teens that I wanted to be a professional golfer.

'I finished my education — my parents insisted on that — and then I turned pro when I was 20. I didn't make it for a while, but eventually I got there.'

'I have always enjoyed team golf, whether it's Leinster Youths, Ireland or Europe in the Ryder Cup.'

'Certainly I would have considered myself to have been stronger at stroke play. It's a completely different game and most professionals are programmed to play 72 holes.

'Winning the European match play kind of changed that perception. I think I had to go through six or seven rounds to win it, and I suppose at the time I really got into it. I didn't play a lot of amateur golf, but I did play through the ranks and I played a lot of match play. I always enjoyed it. I think if you are a competitor and like competition, you will enjoy match play.'

Playing in the Ryder Cup was a dream come true for Des. For as long as he could remember he had wanted to be a professional golfer competing at the highest level, and that meant playing in the Ryder Cup.

'I think any player who comes on tour, whether it's in Europe or America, has the Ryder Cup as a priority. It's certainly something that golfers want to achieve in their careers,' he said.

Des had a decent if unspectacular amateur career. He won the Leinster and Munster Boys' titles in 1969, but a major amateur title eluded him. He did, however, mark himself down as a good team player representing Ireland in the Home Internationals in 1972 and 73 and also competing in the European Amateur Championships in 1973.

'I have always enjoyed team golf, whether it's Leinster Youths, Ireland or Europe in the Ryder Cup,' said Des. 'I was part of the Irish team that won the Dunhill Cup in 1988 — I got such a buzz out of that.

'I like the camaraderie and the friendship of team competition, and I'd like to think I'm the kind of person who can gel well in a team environment. Team events, winning the Dunhill Cup and playing in the Ryder Cup have been highlights of my career.'

The foursomes debacle with Brown and a subsequent singles thrashing at the hands of Hale Irwin failed to dent Des's enthusiasm for team golf in 1979. It whetted his appetite and increased his determination to play

Des Smyth pictured with Gaelic Athletic Association president 2003–2006 Sean Kelly at the announcement that the Ryder Cup would be held from Friday 22 to Sunday 24 September 2006 at the K Club, Co. Kildare.

his way back on to the Ryder Cup team for the 1981 clash at Walton Heath, Surrey.

'I made my mind up after the Greenbrier that I was going to target a place on the team in 1981. I was an improving player and in the end I played my way back on to the team quite comfortably,' he said.

By 1981 Des was an established player on tour, having won twice in 1980 and once again in 1981. He was no longer a rookie plucked from obscurity, and he made sure that returning captain John Jacobs knew exactly where he stood on likely pairings.

'I felt I was a better player in 1981, and I had a long chat with John Jacobs after the 1979 event, so I was more

comfortable going into the Ryder Cup at Walton Heath,' said Des.

'I should have said something in 1979, but I was a rookie and I didn't have the confidence. In 1979 I let the established players, the likes of Bernard Gallacher and Brian Barnes, discuss selections with the captain. I was just happy to be playing.

'In 1981 I felt more was expected of me. I was viewed as a strong player, I was better prepared and I wanted to get some points. I told John which players I wasn't comfortable playing with.'

The European build-up to the event was dogged with controversy over selection issues. Seve Ballesteros, winner of the 1980 Masters title, had fallen out with the European Tour and as a result had not played often enough in Europe to earn his place on the team. His only way into the event was as a wildcard, but the selection committee chose Peter Oosterhuis and Mark James (now forgiven after his problems in 1979).

The Europeans went into the contest without their major winners, Ballesteros or Tony Jacklin, who was also overlooked for a wildcard place. In contrast, the American team had won 36 major titles between them, and is still regarded as one of the greatest teams ever assembled.

'The Seve thing didn't have much impact on the team,' said Des. 'That was an issue between him and the tour and had nothing to do with the rest of us. The team just got on with preparing to play. The Americans looked unbeatable on paper, but we were determined that we could win the match.

'It was a young team and we were full of fire. Faldo, Langer, Lyle and Torrance were all on that team. These guys were on the way up and they proved it subsequently.'

Des proved his worth to the team by winning two points on the opening day of competition. In the morning

Des Smyth and his caddy Ray Latchford during round one of the AIB Irish Seniors Open at the Heritage Golf & Country Club, Killenard, Co. Laois (June 2005).

foursomes, Des and Bernard Gallacher beat Raymond Floyd and Hale Irwin 3 and 2. The Europeans carded five birdies and an eagle on their way to a morale-boosting win over one of America's top pairings.

'Bernard was a very good competitor; he never gave too much away,' said Des. 'It's a special feeling to win your first points in the Ryder Cup. You are never really going to get an easy game in the Ryder Cup and this American team was, on paper, the strongest ever assembled.

'I was also delighted to finally beat Hale Irwin after losing twice to him at the Greenbrier. The team got off to a great start on that first day — it was very exciting.'

The Europeans did indeed make a fantastic start to the contest and finished day one leading by 4½-3½. Des followed up his morning victory by adding a second point in the afternoon partnering José Maria Canizares in the fourballs.

It was a calculated gamble by John Jacobs to pair the two men together, but it worked superbly as they combined to thrash Bill Rogers and Bruce Lietzke 6 and 5. The Europeans finished the first day on a high, but those early defeats only served to sting

the Americans into action, and from the first match on day two they took control, sweeping the European challenge away to complete a crushing 18½-9½ victory.

Des played in every session of the 1981 Ryder Cup but could not repeat his excellence of the opening day, losing three further matches.

'John used to say to me that he played me too few times in 1979 and too often in 81,' said Des. 'I think he is probably right. Five matches is a big ask with all the excitement and tension involved in the Ryder Cup.

'It's tough because the concentration levels are so high. You have to be very confident with your game, or if you're not you have to concentrate hard and try to get the best out of your game.

'It is quite a strain. I never felt tired, but in hindsight you're probably better off, unless the guy is playing fantastic, giving guys a rest. That way they get a rest mentally as opposed to physically.'

The American class and experience eventually overpowered the European resistance at Walton Heath. Des faced rookie Ben Crenshaw in the singles. To emphasise the depth of talent on the teams, Crenshaw had only played once at that stage, losing a fourball match on Friday to Sandy Lyle and Mark James.

The Texan blitzed his Irish opponent with a run of birdies that left him four up after 12 holes on his way to a 6 and 4 victory.

'It's tough because the concentration levels are so high. You have to be very confident with your game.'

Des Smyth pictured during the Murphy's Irish Open at Fota Island Golf Club, Co. Cork (June 2002).

'There was very little I could do about it,' said Des. 'As the week went on my game was not as good as it had been at the start. He rattled off a string of birdies. I played steadily enough, but he was holing putts from all over the place.'

Des finished the event as joint top points scorer for Europe but he failed to force his way on to subsequent Ryder Cup teams.

'I wanted to get on to the team again and, funnily enough, I played my best golf in the late 1980s. I think 1988 was my best year on tour, but I kept playing well in the even years and not during the qualification period,' said Des.

As Europe found direction under Tony Jacklin and then finally broke the American dominance in 1985 at the Belfry, Des was left to sit and watch it all on television.

> **'I never prioritised the Ryder Cup, never started out the year with it in mind. Maybe I should have.'**

'I never really worried about missing out. I'm not that type of person,' said Des. 'I loved watching those Ryder Cups and I supported the boys playing as best I could. I would love to have played on a winning team, but it never really bothered me that much.

'I never prioritised the Ryder Cup, never started out the year with it in mind. Maybe I should have. I thought to myself, I've done that, and just tried to concentrate on my career.'

Chapter 12

Ronan Rafferty

Ronan Rafferty plays from a bunker during the Open Championship at St Andrews (July 1990).

Standing on the 18th tee at the Belfry, Ronan Rafferty was weighing up the value of taking the safe route to the fairway below. He was all square with his tormentor from the previous two days, Mark Calcavecchia.

The reigning Open champion had already racked up two foursomes victories over Ronan on Friday and Saturday. Drawn against him again in the singles, the Warrenpoint man had been handed the chance of redemption, but he needed to be positive.

'I was desperately nervous,' said Ronan. 'I considered taking the safe line to the right, but then I decided to be brave.'

Ronan Rafferty in action.

Ronan hit a mammoth drive that carried 250 yards over trees and water before landing in the fairway only a mid-iron from the green. In fact, Ronan's drive almost hit American Payne Stewart who was playing in the match ahead.

Stewart had found the Belfry's famous lake off the tee and had somehow hacked his ball out from the water's edge on to the fairway. He was contemplating his third shot when Ronan's drive bounced past him.

As a result, Calcavecchia, who had been ready to drive, was forced to wait for what probably seemed like an eternity. The delay did him no favours. With his opponent well placed and the match on the line, the American stepped up to his ball and skied his drive straight into the lake.

Taking a penalty drop, he was forced to gamble and instead of pitching short of the stream that fronted the green, he went for the putting surface and for a second time dumped his shot into the water.

There was no way back and the American walked round to join Ronan in the fairway where he promptly conceded the match without the Irishman having to hit another shot.

'From what I had seen of Ronan's ability over the previous 17 holes, I knew he wasn't going to dump that one in the water,' said the Open champion. 'Rafferty is no superman, but only super golf will beat him.'

● ● ● ●

There was never any doubt that Ronan Rafferty would one day play in the Ryder Cup. The question was simply a matter of 'when' as opposed to 'if'.

A product of Warrenpoint Golf Club in Co. Down, Ronan was a golfing prodigy and from an early age was tipped to take his place among the greats of the game. He had a solid all-round game, but it was his crisp iron play and mature course management that set him apart from his contemporaries.

afterwards and although he failed to win his European tour card at qualifying school, he performed well enough on the Safari circuit in Africa over the winter to book his place on the tour.

In 1982, his first full season as a professional, he won the Venezuelan Open, but his progression stalled and it would be a further five years before Ronan returned to the winner's enclosure.

The catalyst for his re-emergence seemed to be his marriage to Clare in 1987. The pair spent four months on honeymoon together in Australia, during which time he won three events including the New Zealand Open. He returned to Europe in 1988 with renewed

> He finished the 1988 season in ninth place on the order of merit. More importantly, he was also well placed in the Ryder Cup table.

Jack Magowan, golf journalist with the *Belfast Telegraph*, compared Ronan's iron play with that of the legendary Fred Daly. 'He was excellent with a long iron in his hands,' said Jack, 'a wonderful crisp striker.'

Daly himself admired the young professional's ability. 'I once asked Fred what was the difference between Rafferty and himself. Ronan would have been 21 at the time,' said Jack. 'Fred said that when he had a seven-iron in his hand he was looking to hit the green, whereas Ronan was unhappy if he finished more than 12 feet from the hole.'

Ronan was playing off scratch at 15, the year he won the British Boys' title. Two years later he played on the Walker Cup team that lost 15-9 to the Americans at Cypress Point, California. He turned pro shortly

focus and put together a superb year which he capped by helping Ireland to victory over Australia, in the final of the Dunhill Cup at St Andrews.

That first European Tour victory still eluded him, but the Dunhill Cup triumph convinced him that it was just a matter of time and patience. Speaking sometime later in *The Irish Times* he said: 'That breakthrough (the Dunhill Cup) seemed to set me up for a wonderful run.' He finished the 1988 season in ninth place on the order of merit. More importantly, he was also well placed in the Ryder Cup table.

'A Ryder Cup blazer is my first goal this year,' he said as the 1989 season got under way. 'I'll not be happy, however, until I've banked over £125,000. Then I'll know I'm in the team for certain.'

He needn't have worried. As the season got started the Warrenpoint man stepped his game up to another level. Throughout 1989 Rafferty was far and away Europe's most consistent golfer, putting together a string of top-ten finishes that jetted him up the money list and into first place on the Ryder Cup table.

Every week it seemed that he was going to break his European Tour duck, and finally in May he claimed the Italian Open. The victory, coming on the back of his blistering early season form, practically guaranteed him a place on the team to face the US at the Belfry.

'This is what I wanted most,' he said. 'I said before the season began that I didn't deserve to make the Belfry unless I won a tournament. It might have put extra pressure on me but I meant it. Certainly this victory is a ton weight off my shoulders'

A couple of weeks later Ronan chased Nick Faldo home in the British Masters at Woburn, prompting the Englishman to say: 'He (Ronan) has matured into a very good player and kept me on my toes all afternoon. He can go any time to be fitted for a Ryder Cup blazer.'

Ronan maintained his form throughout the rest of the summer and claimed a second tour victory in August when he won the Scandinavian Open with a final round 65.

Ronan Rafferty *(extreme left)* **pictured with Ryder Cup team mates Christy O'Connor Jnr** *(centre)* **and Jose Maria Olazabal at the Belfry (September 1989).**

At that stage the Ryder Cup couldn't come quickly enough for him. It was his time. He was 25 years old, playing the best golf of his career, and he was soon to become a father for the first time. A few weeks before the start of the Ryder Cup, Clare gave birth to their first child, Jonathan.

Ronan topped the Ryder Cup points table when the European team was announced at the conclusion of the German Open in late August. More importantly, from captain Tony Jacklin's point of view, he was the only rookie in a side which included familiar names like Nick Faldo, Seve Ballesteros and José Maria Olazabal.

Jacklin, in his fourth and final match in charge, plumped for experience when making his three wildcard choices, selecting Howard Clark, Bernhard Langer and, surprisingly, Christy O'Connor Jnr. That meant no place for another Irishman, Philip Walton, who actually finished ahead of Christy in the Ryder Cup points table. 'Christy is a cool cookie and very experienced,' said Ronan, on hearing of Junior's selection. 'I thought, as most fans at home probably did, that Walton might have made it, but we're all happy for Christy.'

In contrast to the Europeans, US captain Raymond Floyd didn't have the luxury of experience to rely on. Two successive Ryder Cup defeats had shaken American golf, and Floyd was going into the match with five rookies in his side. Paul Azinger, Chip Beck, Fred Couples, Ken Green and Mark McCumber were all newcomers to the event, having qualified as of right.

Floyd had been handed two wildcard picks when he took over as captain, and he was forced to bring in some much-needed experience in the shape of Tom Watson and Lanny Wadkins. Of the two captains, Floyd was clearly under the greater pressure, and the team flew to England with the words of President George Bush ringing in their ears, 'Don't come back without the cup.'

American attitudes towards the competition were changing after back-to-back defeats, a fact recognised by Tom Watson. 'It (losing) spurred us on to think more seriously about the Ryder Cup as a matter of national pride, rather than a social exercise,' he said.

Consequently, Floyd promised to take a hard-line approach with his team. 'I will not ask a player if there is somebody he would like to play with. I will tell him,' said Floyd.

'I've been on teams where we had guys who acted like their feelings were hurt because they didn't get to play with a certain colleague. I won't have that. My function is to pick the pairings; the players' duty is to compete.'

The Americans may well have been inexperienced, but they still had world-class stars like Curtis Strange and Tom Kite to call on. Ronan felt it was not going to be easy for the Europeans to retain the trophy.

'They (the US team) are here to try and shut us up,' he said. 'They're bent on restoring lost pride and we are just as determined to stop them. It'll be a tough match and an exciting one. The cup belongs here, however, and here it stays.'

Practice went reasonably well for Ronan, who partnered German Bernhard Langer in final practice sessions. There had been some thoughts among the assembled

'I said before the season began that I didn't deserve to make the Belfry unless I won a tournament.'

media that Ronan would play with Howard Clark as both men used the same make of ball, but Jacklin felt Ronan needed an experienced hand to guide him.

'Ronan has become a very fine player, but one must still be aware that this is his first Ryder Cup,' Jacklin said. 'He needs the sort of experience that a player like Langer can provide.'

Ronan was looking forward to the challenge of competing in the event and completing his set of representative honours, having already played in the Walker Cup, the World Cup, the Dunhill Cup and the Kirin Cup.

'It is an emotional landmark in my career,' he said. 'Obviously this team is special and it is great to know that I deserve to be here. I never wanted to become a Ryder Cup player until I had proved my worth by winning a European tournament.'

and Rafferty was a bit of a mismatch. 'To be honest, I don't know that there really was anybody Ronan could have played with in the foursomes,' Dryden stated. He cited a lack of communication as a key contributing factor to what turned out to be a scrappy, disjointed performance by the Europeans.

Calcavecchia and Green, good friends off the course, grabbed an early lead with birdies on the 1st and 2nd. The Americans, who played untidily themselves, held a three-hole lead as they turned for home. They bogeyed the 11th and 13th, but the Europeans also bogeyed the 12th to leave the gap at two.

The match appeared to be slipping away from the Europeans, but they were handed a lifeline on the par five 15th when the Americans dumped their second shot into the ditch that ran across the fairway. Unbelievably, Langer then followed the Americans into the same ditch. The hole was halved in double-bogey seven and

> ## 'I never wanted to become a Ryder Cup player until I had proved my worth by winning a European tournament.'

He added: 'I think people have been rather flattering in their assessment of me as a player. I've yet to convince myself about my own play, though I have obviously made considerable advancement this season.'

All the improvement in the world couldn't prepare Ronan for the nerves associated with hitting his opening tee-shot in the Ryder Cup. In his first appearance he had the dubious honour of getting his foursomes match against Calcavecchia and Green off and running.

Caddie Stuart Dryden claims that Ronan was so nervous he was simply delighted to make contact with the ball. Commenting in Norman Dabel's *How We Won the Ryder Cup*, the caddie also felt the pairing of Langer

the Americans went on to put the Europeans out of their misery with a 2 and 1 victory. Jack Magowan, writing in the *Belfast Telegraph*, stated: 'Langer was at war with his game, the weak link in the partnership.'

It was a depressing start for Ronan. He hadn't actually played too badly, but the pairing simply hadn't worked. Unfortunately, he was left out of the afternoon fourballs so there was no way he could get straight back in to rectify the situation. Instead, Jacklin sent Ronan out for an afternoon practice round with Christy O'Connor, who had been left out of the opening day action. It hinted at an end to the Langer/Rafferty pairing, and a few hours later the Irishmen were named to play in the foursomes on day two.

Ronan Rafferty *(right)* **chats with Ryder Cup team mate Gordon Brand Jnr (September 1989).**

Ronan Rafferty (*back row, second from right*) **celebrates Europe's Ryder Cup victory over America. Also included is Christy O'Connor Jnr** (*front row, extreme left*) **(September 1989).**

'I thought something like this might happen, but I honestly didn't know until Tony told me at tea-time,' said Christy. 'Where team selection is concerned, he keeps his cards very close to his chest.'

Dermot Gilleece, writing in *The Irish Times*, said: 'The recall of the Ulsterman would suggest that Jacklin recognised the greater weakness of Langer in their defeat by Mark Calcavecchia and Ken Green.'

Ronan's defeat aside, it had been a superb opening day for Europe, who swept the afternoon fourballs 4-0 to take a 5-3 lead into day two.

'I've just had an eyeball-to-eyeball talk with my team and they are shell-shocked. Me too for that matter,' said Floyd. 'I just cannot explain it. On paper my boys should have won the fourball series by the same margin (3-1) that they did the foursomes. Instead, they got dumped with the empties 4-0. I still can't believe it.'

By naming Ronan in the foursomes on day two, Jacklin was clearly banking on Europe's No. 1 golfer to show the kind of form that had swept him to the top of the Ryder Cup points table. Unfortunately, Ronan was clearly finding the Ryder Cup environment an intimidating one. He was nervous, and when he and

Christy tackled Green and Calcavecchia the nerves of both players became particularly apparent on the greens.

Christy felt it was a poor pairing and that both he and Ronan should have been paired with more experienced men. As it turned out, Ronan was involved in another partnership that simply failed to click.

'With Christy they played quite nicely from tee to green, but when they got on the green it was just diabolical,' said Dryden. 'They were just trying to roll the ball down to the holeside, but it managed to roll two or three feet past. They must have missed half a dozen two or three-footers.'

Saturday evening, stating that he wasn't 'comfortable about playing'. Jacklin pointed out that it was going to be difficult for Ronan to get out of the singles and tried his best to encourage the rookie.

'I knew he was unhappy with his foursomes effort,' said Jacklin. 'So I said to him at breakfast on Sunday, you're too good a player not to score a point this week. Go out there and do your stuff.'

Jacklin's pep-talk seemed to have the desired effect, and Dryden noticed that his man was more composed as they waited to get their singles match against Calcavecchia under way.

> **'You're too good a player not to score a point this week. Go out there and do your stuff.'**

The Irish pair started confidently enough, with Christy rolling in a nine-footer for a birdie which was matched by Calcavecchia a few moments later. The Europeans went one up following an American bogey at the 2nd but were all square again after a dropped shot at the 3rd.

In a fluctuating encounter the Americans led by three at the turn after the Europeans contrived to three-putt from 20 feet. At the short par four 10th Ronan, going for the green, found the burn surrounding the green, while Calcavecchia and Green recorded an eagle to go four up.

By the 12th the Americans had extended that lead to five and even though the Europeans fought back with birdies on the 13th and 15th, it was a case of too little too late, and the Americans ran out comfortable 3 and 2 winners.

A second defeat in a row was a real dent to Ronan's fragile confidence and he sought out Jacklin on

After splitting the day two matches 4-4, Europe needed 5½ points from the remaining 12 singles ties. The Ulsterman hit his opening drive straight down the middle and proceeded to birdie the opening three holes to leap into a two-hole lead. Calcavecchia fought back, winning the 5th with a birdie and the 6th with a par after Ronan pulled his tee-shot into the water. Ronan refused to be rattled by conceding his lead and birdied the 9th to be out in 33 with a one-hole lead.

The American won the 10th after finding the green with his tee-shot and then took the lead for the first time in the match after Ronan three-putted the 12th. Ronan responded straight away by holing an eight foot birdie putt on the 13th to level matters again.

The next three holes were halved in regulation, leaving the outcome of the match resting on the final two holes. At the 17th Calcavecchia had a ten foot putt to win the hole, but the ball stayed above ground and with the hole halved in par fives the two players moved to the

18th tee, where it all went disastrously wrong for the American.

Ronan's victory was one of only five recorded by the Europeans as they failed to gather the required 5½ points to win the trophy. Christy O'Connor also claimed a famous victory over Fred Couples, but defeats for the last four Europeans left the teams tied on 14 points each. Europe, as holders, retained the cup and Jacklin made a point of singling out Rafferty for his performance.

'It was wonderful to see the way he responded,' said Jacklin. 'One can easily forget that he is only 25 and

> **'One can easily forget that he is only 25 and by his own admission he encountered the greatest pressure of his young career.'**

by his own admission he encountered the greatest pressure of his young career, greater even than facing the 18th green in the British Open.'

Ronan returned to tournament golf after the Ryder Cup with the intention of finishing the season as Europe's No. 1 golfer. He did so in emphatic style by winning the Volvo Masters in October. He deservedly finished the year in first place with European Tour winnings of over £400,000. He would go on to become Ireland's first golfer to break the £1 million barrier.

Subsequently, he never managed to again reach the heights of 1989, and a mixture of injury and poor play kept him out of future Ryder Cup sides. His last European Tour victory was the Austrian Open in 1993. Since then he has played fitfully on tour. As golf gradually takes a back seat, Ronan has been developing a career as a golf commentator with Sky Sports.

Ronan Rafferty surveys the putting surface from a greenside bunker.

Chapter 13
David Feherty

David Feherty prepares to play from the 1st fairway during the Open Championship at Turnberry (July 1994).

If David Feherty needed further proof that he was in real trouble, he only had to look around him.

Moments earlier the crowd had been simply hysterical, now they were almost frenzied as the US Open champion Payne Stewart staged a late fight back. Four up with five to play, David had been coasting to a famous Ryder Cup singles victory when Stewart suddenly found some form. Dragging his game together he had engineered wins at the 15th and 16th to give him hope of an unlikely half.

David Feherty plays from the sand during the Ryder Cup at Kiawah Island (September 1991).

'**P**ayne was a great friend of mine,' said David. (Stewart died in a plane crash in October 1999.)

'The Calcavecchia collapse was happening behind me (four up with four to play, the former British Open champion fell apart and halved his match with Colin Montgomerie) and all I could think about was, was this going to happen to me?

'At one stage I was four up with four to play. It was probably the greatest round of golf I had ever played. I was totally absorbed by the game. I wasn't even feeling particularly nervous. I was caught up in actually doing it, freed from the burden of responsibility — in the zone. Then all of a sudden I lost two in a row.

He should have, but he didn't. Instead, he launched a 'blind' (his words) one-iron that finished inside his opponent's ball. When Stewart's birdie putt slipped by the hole, David was able to nudge his putt up to the edge to secure a remarkable Ryder Cup point.

'The worst I ever felt with a golf club in my hand was on the 17th tee at the Ocean Course at Kiawah Island', he wrote later. 'Payne Stewart had hit a fabulous shot on to the green, which to me by this stage looked about the size of my ball. The club felt extremely light in my hands and I experienced giddiness as I teed the ball up.

'I can honestly say that I have no recollection of the swing I made. I don't remember how it felt, how the ball flew or, for that matter, how I even made contact.

> ## 'I was trying to get to the 17th tee after losing the 16th. It was like trying to fight your way through a riot.'

'I was trying to get to the 17th tee after losing the 16th. It was like trying to fight your way through a riot. The crowd was just wild. They sort of half-cleared a path for me to get through, but then this lady marshal — she must have thought I was a spectator or something — stepped out in front of me and said: "Where do you think you're going?"

'It was the perfect opportunity for Payne to walk past me and watch me lose my mind, but he didn't. He stopped and put his arm around me. He said, "Ma'am, I'd love you to stop him here, but he's playing against me", and he just sort of swept me up on to the tee. Mind you, the bastard then hit a three-wood on to the green.'

That should have been David Feherty's cue to buckle under the pressure. A Ryder Cup rookie, born and raised in Bangor, Co. Down, he should have gone the way of countless others that week and dumped his ball in the water fronting the green.

The only thing I remember is turning around to see European captain Bernard Gallacher, his arms outstretched towards me, and former captain Tony Jacklin facing backwards with his hands over his eyes.

'Apparently Tony had even less faith in me than I did. The ball finished about 30 feet left of the hole and I won the match 2 and 1. That much I do remember.'

• • • •

If CBS Sports ever secure the rights to screen the Ryder Cup, David Feherty will have to go AWOL. As one of America's foremost on-course commentators, his ready wit has earned him a legion of fans. That support might disappear if he was forced to commentate on the Ryder Cup.

'I'd be flamingly biased,' he claims. 'I did cover the opening day at Sam's (Torrance) Ryder Cup at the

Belfry in 2002. It's an NBC show, but I got a special dispensation for that one day. It's something I knew I would never do again. And I will *never* do it again. First of all I was too hung over to be on television, and secondly I was way too involved.'

David has a genuine passion for the Ryder Cup. That's not surprising when you consider that his best friend is Sam Torrance, a man synonymous with the event, and

it, they feel the pressure, and that generates the tension and the incredible atmosphere.'

The Ryder Cup first seeped into David's consciousness in 1969 when Jack Nicklaus guaranteed Tony Jacklin a half by conceding a two foot putt on the 18th green at Royal Birkdale. That famous gesture by Nicklaus, playing in his first Ryder Cup, ensured that the match was tied for the first time in over 30 years. Twelve

> **'Playing in the Ryder Cup is about marking your territory, bragging rights, why you start playing the game in the first place.'**

that he was competing at a time when the matches were at their most intense. Europe, driven on by the likes of Seve, Langer and Faldo, were flexing their muscles and striving to make up for years of hurt and humiliation at the hands of numerous US teams. The Ryder Cup was developing into the huge sporting event that it is today, and David was stuck in the middle, loving every second of it.

'Playing in the Ryder Cup is about marking your territory, bragging rights, why you start playing the game in the first place,' he added. 'It's hard to put into words, but there's almost a childlike thing to it. It's a form of one-upmanship. There's no other golf event in the world that can make you feel like the Ryder Cup can, and that's even just watching it.

'You can see how it affects the players. They don't act the same as they do in a major championship. You don't see them punching the air if they hit a green with a seven-iron in the third round of a normal event, but they do in the Ryder Cup, and every hole is like that. It affects the crowd in a similar way. They see the magnitude of

years on from the victory at Lindrick, GB & I finally had something to cheer about, and golf was back in the limelight.

It was big news and David Feherty, 11 years old at the time, was enthralled by it. America soon regained their stranglehold on the event, but the Ryder Cup had a new fan. His golfing heroes were the Ryder Cup stars of the day, people like Arnold Palmer, Jack Nicklaus, Brian Barnes and Peter Oosterhuis.

He loved the game and was a regular feature around Bangor Golf Club, where he fell under the watchful eye of former tour player, David Jones. He practised hard and continued to improve, but he was not an exceptional talent and his decision to turn professional at 17 stunned many people. He was a five handicapper at the time and a good student who had no background in top-level amateur golf. It was a wild shot in the dark but one that Jones supported.

'Everyone said he was mad,' said Jones.

David Feherty tees off during the Epson Grand Prix of Europe at the St Pierre Golf Club (May 1989).

'I said, don't worry. He'll get there because of his desire. His ability to work was quite astonishing.'

Unsurprisingly, David struggled initially to make the grade as a professional. He failed at the tour school three years in succession from 1977 to 1979 but remained committed to his cause, and he found the camaraderie of life on tour to his liking. He continued to work hard and embarked on a long apprenticeship, one that mixed a stint as David Jones's caddie with regular appearances on the Sunshine Tour in Africa and a job as assistant pro at Balmoral Golf Club, the home of Fred Daly. In many ways it was the perfect place for David.

Eddie Polland, a Ryder Cup player in 1973, was attached to the club, while Fred, Ireland's only Open winner, was a veteran of four cup encounters.

'He loved telling stories about the players he competed with and against in the Ryder Cup, people like Henry

Cotton and Ken Bousfield,' said David. 'I never really worked with Fred but I played with him. Fred wasn't great at explaining how to play golf, but he sure as hell could show you.'

Gradually the hard work started to pay off and in 1984 David claimed his first victory of any note when he won the ICL International in South Africa. The following year he made his debut for Ireland in the Dunhill Cup. He had finally arrived.

'I never felt that my lack of top-level amateur experience was a problem when it came to team golf,' said David. 'In my career my best golf was played in team events whether that was the World Cup, the Dunhill Cup or the Ryder Cup. I always seemed to play my best in team events. I don't know why. It was probably because I had support. There was safety in numbers.'

In 1986 David made his big breakthrough on the European Tour, winning twice. His victories in the

David Feherty acknowledges the fans after holing out during the Ryder Cup at Kiawah Island (September 1991).

Italian Open and later the Bell's Scottish Open put him into contention for a possible Ryder Cup debut.

'I didn't qualify for the 1987 team, but I began to think that maybe I might be able to make the team,' he said. 'It had always seemed like a dream, unattainable.'

While fellow Irishmen Eamonn Darcy and Christy O'Connor Jnr were being fêted for their roles in the 1987 and 89 victories, David was battling to find the consistency necessary to book his place on the team. He continued to win, he competed in major championships (finishing fourth in the 1989 British Open), but it wasn't until the end of the 1990 season that he finally found the resolve required to make the team.

event which at times threatened to get out of control. The course ran along the coastline and the cross-winds made it almost impossible to control the ball.

'It was so difficult it was possible to drop a shot between the locker room and the 1st tee', wrote David.

'It was unlike anything on our side of the water', he added. 'It looked like a links course, but the greens were built up in the air, and hard. They were pretty unhittable in terms of running a shot up, like on a links. You had to try and fly it up there and then the wind blew it away. At that stage in my career it was the hardest golf course I had ever played.'

> # 'It looked like a links course, but the greens were built up in the air, and hard.'

David reeled off a number of top-ten finishes and then captained Ireland to a famous Dunhill Cup victory over the old enemy, England, at St Andrews. He maintained his form as the 1991 season got under way, finishing second in the Catalonia Open in March and then in May he won the Credit Lyonnais in France.

By the time he finished fifth in August's Scandinavian Masters, he was already a confirmed member of the side which would tackle the US over the Ocean Course at Kiawah Island.

Kiawah was a new development and had not been the original choice to host the 1991 event. That honour had gone to the PGA West in California, but television concerns forced the PGA of America to switch the event to accommodate European viewers who did not want to be watching golf in the early hours of the morning. Designed by Pete Dye, the course and its difficulty proved to be one of the major talking points of an

The course was one problem; the animosity between some of the players was an entirely different matter, and one that only served to hype the event to new levels. America had not held the cup for six years and with the Gulf War stoking patriotic fervour, the Ryder Cup descended into the 'War on the Shore'.

New European captain Bernard Gallacher must have wondered what he had got himself into. His team had a familiar and experienced look, with major winners Olazabal, Ballesteros and Faldo being joined by four rookies, David Gilford, Colin Montgomerie, Steven Richardson and David Feherty.

On the US side, captain Dave Stockton was relying on nine men who had previous Ryder Cup experience. Alongside Hale Irwin, Fred Couples and Raymond Floyd were three rookies, Wayne Levi, Steve Pate and leading money winner Corey Pavin.

With a punishing course to navigate, a hostile crowd and some early morning crank phone calls disrupting preparation, a rookie could easily have been swept away, but the European rookies were helped and supported by their more experienced team mates.

In David's case, the whole adventure was made easier by his close friendship with Ryder Cup veteran Sam Torrance.

'It was quite an experience for a Ryder Cup rookie to walk off the world's most beautiful aircraft (Concorde) and into the media maelstrom that had by then become a rivalry of cross-global proportions', wrote David.

'It's like childbirth: it doesn't matter how many times it's described to you, you still have no idea what it's actually like, and I for one was blissfully unaware. During that week Sam made me feel bigger and better and more important than I ever had. He, Bernard Gallacher and the veterans on the team gave me and

afternoon fourballs against Lanny Wadkins and Mark O'Meara. 'Sam and I were good friends with both Lanny and Mark, but for the next five hours we had to be enemies, and I had a problem with that,' added David.

'It's hard to act like a tough guy when every part of your body is shaking. I held up okay until I got to the 1st green. By then it became obvious that putting was going to be a problem. I kind of scuffed the putt up to about four feet and three feet left of the hole.

'Sam made the putt and on the way to the next tee comforted me with the words, "If you don't pull yourself together, I'm going to join them and you can play all three of us, you useless bastard!"'

The European pair trailed by three at the turn, but David brought them back into the match by chipping in for a birdie at the 11th and then holing a nasty six-footer for birdie at the par three 14th. They halved the

> **'It's like childbirth: it doesn't matter how many times it's described to you, you still have no idea what it's actually like.'**

the other rookies a sense that we were part of a special club, a brotherhood if you like. It's a feeling that lasts a lifetime.'

The morning foursomes got under way after a fog delay and right from the start America's Paul Azinger and Europe's Seve Ballesteros locked horns, setting the tone for the entire three days. Azinger and Chip Beck were eventually beaten by Seve and José Maria Olazabal, but that was the only defeat the US suffered as they took the series 3-1.

Both David and Sam sat out the morning's play, but Gallacher paired them together at the top of the

next three holes and in the gathering gloom David was left with an 11 foot putt on the 18th to halve the tie.

'I asked Sam to aim me. To his eternal credit, he said, "Hit it firm on the left edge", in a manner that made me feel he was completely positive', wrote David.

'Somehow I made a controlled spasm and the ball rolled into the centre of the cup. The crowd roared; I almost fainted. Sam and I had made my first Ryder Cup half-point.'

The European team fought back in the afternoon and at the end of day one the Americans had a narrow

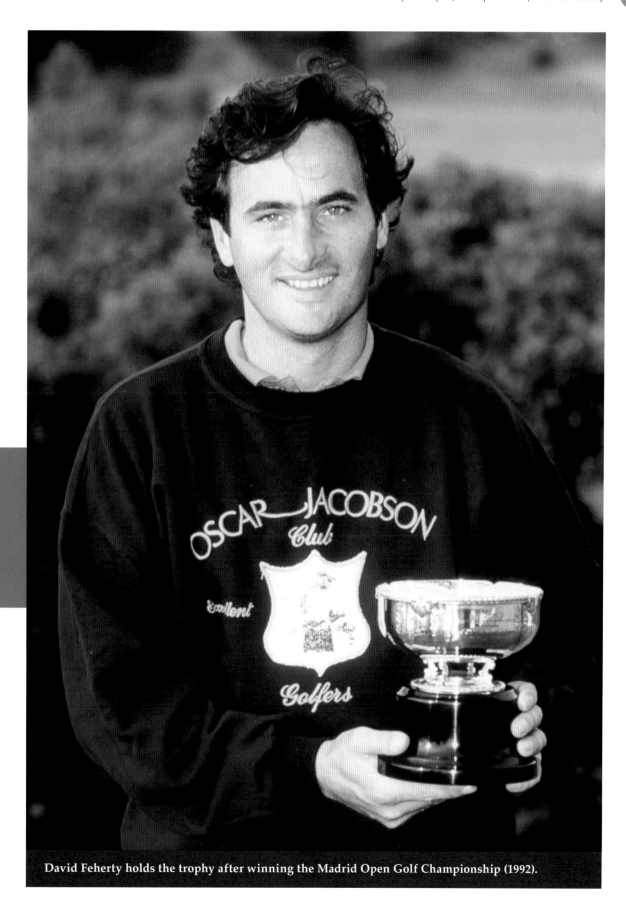

David Feherty holds the trophy after winning the Madrid Open Golf Championship (1992).

4½-3½ lead. The battling half by Feherty and Torrance convinced Gallacher that the pair deserved another chance and he pitched them back into the fray on day two against Hale Irwin and Lanny Wadkins.

In the morning foursomes David and Sam led by one after six holes, but the sides were level at the turn. The Americans got back in front with wins at the 11th and 12th before a short-range par putt from David at the 13th cut the gap to one. Unfortunately, mistakes at the next two holes gifted Irwin and Wadkins a three-hole lead and they closed the match out on the 16th.

'To have Sam as a partner for my two matches was a tremendous help for me,' said David. 'Most of the great moments in my career were his wins, and that includes the Ryder Cup in 2002. I remember when he won the Irish Open, there's a picture of him just picking me up. I weighed about 165 lbs then. He couldn't do that now!

'It was the end of an era when he retired in 2004. He was a torch carrier for the guys who also managed to be one of the boys and still play at the highest level.'

Both David and Sam sat out the afternoon fourballs as Europe bounced back from a poor morning to level the match at 8-8 with just the singles to come. David's caddie at the time, Rod Wooler, remembers how confident David was ahead of his singles clash with Payne, but only after some extensive work on the putting green.

'All week David was hitting the ball fantastically well but struggling with the pace on the greens, struggling with his putting in general,' said Rod. 'We practised the putting for hours each night. By the time we finished on Saturday night, Dave had got it right.'

Out second behind Nick Faldo, who was playing Raymond Floyd, David was gifted an early lead when

David Feherty plays from a bunker during the opening round of the Open Championship at St Andrews (July 1995).

Stewart, who looked nervous, made a mess of the opening four holes. Stewart birdied the 6th to cut the lead to two, but David hit back on the 11th by holing a tricky 12-footer for par to get back to three up.

Four down with four to play, the US Open champion finally responded and cut the gap, but David held himself together long enough to close out the match at the 17th.

'I got behind the eight ball early and hit some bad shots,' said Stewart. 'I kept beating myself. He played better than I did, so he deserves to win.'

David's remarkable victory had helped Europe take two and half points out of the first three matches. The match looked to be swinging in their favour.

'Once you're done playing in the Ryder Cup, you don't even think about what you've done, regardless of whether you've won or lost,' added David. 'All you're thinking about is getting back out as far as you can on the course to watch the lads play until it's over.'

As the singles matches progressed, the Americans stemmed the European onslaught and the outcome of the match came down to the final tie between Bernhard Langer and Hale Irwin on the last green. With both teams crowded round the green, Langer was left with a six foot putt for a half, which would have kept the cup in Europe.

Trying to avoid spike marks on his line, Langer hit his putt firmly towards the left centre of the cup, but the ball slipped agonisingly past the right of the hole. America had won the trophy 14½-13½.

That nerve-tingling finale cemented the Ryder Cup's reputation as one of the world's great sporting events, yet David was unsure whether he wanted to be a part of it in the future.

'You know, even at that stage I was thinking about turning to journalism,' said David. 'In 1993 I just missed out on making the team and I was bitterly disappointed. I was there watching and although part of me wanted to play, I could see even then that I wouldn't be playing golf for the rest of my professional life.'

After the glory years of the early 90s David made the move to America and started competing on the US Tour. He tried to change his game to cope with the 'target golf' style of American courses but failed to make any headway and he retired from competitive golf in 1997, moving into journalism and broadcasting with CBS Sports.

'You know, the Ryder Cup is one of the last pure sporting events left,' he said. 'Money means nothing. It's all about touching that cup. You never stop being a Ryder Cup player. Look at what I do now. I was never a major winner but being a Ryder Cup player is playing at the highest level and that means a lot in terms of street credibility with regard to what you say on air. You are a member of a pretty exclusive club.

'I've been to every Ryder Cup since 1991 and I'll continue to go to them. It's almost a ritual now. It's kind of like being an alcoholic. There's no cure for it.'

'The Ryder Cup is one of the last pure sporting events left. Money means nothing. It's all about touching that cup.'

Chapter 14

Philip Walton

Philip Walton plays from a bunker during practice at Oak Hill (September 1995).

It took a long while for Philip Walton to realise that the outcome of the 1995 Ryder Cup at Oak Hill rested on his shoulders.

He was leading Jay Haas by two holes with two left to play when he noticed the huge galleries following his match.

'With so many people around as I walked up the 17th, I had a feeling it had all come down to my match,' said Philip. 'And I was sure of it when I looked at the scoreboard. And I thought, I didn't want this but I'm going to make the best of it.'

Philip Walton is lifted off his feet by European captain Bernard Gallacher after holing the putt that won the Ryder Cup at Oak Hill, Rochester, New York (September 1995).

Philip had been cruising along against Haas until the 16th.

He had started the match brightly, leading by two after two holes before Haas clawed him back to level after six.

The Dubliner responded to Haas's fight back by taking control of the match. He regained his two-hole lead and then fired a brilliant six-iron into the 15th green which stopped four feet from the hole. When he rolled in the putt for a winning birdie, it seemed like the man from Malahide was on his way to a glorious victory.

As they marched up the 16th, Philip's caddie Bryan McLauchlan was trying not to think too far ahead.

'Philip played 16 beautifully. Down the left-hand side, plonks it on the middle of the green — lovely. Jay misses the green right and goes in the trap. Surely it's all over now?' he said.

'Haas slashes out — and into the hole! Well, there's nothing we can do about that. Okay. No big problem. We're still two up with two to play. No problem.'

But there was a problem. For the first time in the match Philip was, understandably in the circumstances, feeling the pressure. He played a beautiful chip and run on to the 17th green, leaving himself a four-footer to win the hole and the match, but his putt caught the left lip and spun out.

Haas won the hole with a par and felt the match had turned his way.

'After winning the 16th and 17th I felt I had the momentum to get the half-point we needed,' said the American. 'Everything was going to plan.'

The same could not be said for Philip, who later admitted that he couldn't feel his legs as he stood on the 18th tee.

Haas needed to get a good drive away to pile the pressure back on the Irishman but, clearly suffering from nerves himself, he proceeded to hit a dreadful short hook which finished in the rough behind a tree.

Philip's drive wasn't much better. He pushed it right into the rough but short of a fairway bunker. He was, however, in a much better position than Haas, who could only punch his second out into the fairway.

Philip went for the green with his second, hitting a five-wood from the rough, but it came up short finishing in thick rough on a bank in front of the green.

However, the advantage remained with the Irishman after Haas's third, from the middle of the fairway, pitched on the green and spun back on to the fringe from where he chipped eight feet past the hole.

Left with a tricky shot from the rough, Philip, using a technique he picked up from Ian Woosnam, played a lovely chip to 10 feet and from there he two-putted for a remarkable victory.

'He (Philip) was at the bottom of the field where all the heat was on and never shirked his responsibility,' said European captain Bernard Gallacher. 'But they were the longest two putts I have ever had to watch.'

'Philip played 16 beautifully. Down the left-hand side, plonks it on the middle of the green.'

• • • •

There's a well-known golf cliché: 'it's not how, but how many', and for Philip Walton that was particularly true of the 18th at Oak Hill.

He and Jay Haas hacked their way up the last, but in the end it was Walton's nerve that held under the greatest pressure imaginable. It was a truly fantastic display from a man who was clearly concerned about his ability to handle the stress of a Ryder Cup.

Philip had spent most of the 1995 season trying not to think or even talk about the Ryder Cup. He even went so far as to dismiss his interest in the event after winning the Irish Professional Championship in May.

'I'm not interested in the Ryder Cup. It's producing so much pressure that players are being destroyed,' he said.

His statement caused some consternation among the press, coming just three weeks after his second European Tour victory at the Catalan Open put him right in the mix for a debut at Oak Hill.

'He wanted to get the press off his back and he was dead right,' said the Scot in *The Irish Times*. 'For a year, from the first round of the first qualifying tournament last September, I've had questions about the Ryder Cup after every round. You get too much of it and Philip didn't want that. He wanted to be on the team as much as any of us, but without all the hassle. It worked.'

Philip was perfectly within his rights to laugh off the prospect of Ryder Cup qualification. In 1989 he experienced the heartbreak of missing out by the narrowest of margins after Tony Jacklin plumped for Christy O'Connor Jnr as one of his wildcards, despite the fact that Philip had finished ahead of him in the Ryder Cup standings.

At the time Jacklin stated: 'Philip Walton was very much in my thoughts, but these are difficult decisions that I have to live with. Walton has a great opportunity of getting into future teams — he's a young player of tremendous promise.'

It had taken Philip a long time to get over the disappointment of missing out in 1989 and he refused, at least in public, to let the 1995 season be dictated by

'I knew I now had the opportunity of wiping out the memory of that disappointment in Frankfurt.'

He later claimed he had been joking and there probably was a fair degree of 'tongue in cheek' involved in that statement, because Philip dearly wanted to play in the Ryder Cup. He just didn't want to deal with the constant media speculation involved with making the team.

Sam Torrance, a member of the 1995 team at Oak Hill and later European captain in 2002 at the Belfry, clearly felt Philip had taken the right approach.

dreams of Ryder Cup selection. Privately, as Philip later revealed in *The Irish Times*, he had put a place on the 1995 Ryder Cup team top of his wish list as the season got under way.

'I told my friends at the start of the year that I knew this would be my season. I was prepared to wager £1,000 that I would qualify for the Ryder Cup side and win two tournaments. I wanted odds of 20-1, but nobody would take the bet,' he said.

'After shooting 66 at Portmarnock on a wild, winter's day, with eight birdies and two bogeys, I woke up the following morning and felt deep down in my bones that it was all going to happen for me. Though I hadn't yet reached my 33rd birthday, I suddenly felt as if I was running out of time.

'I knew I now had the opportunity of wiping out the memory of that disappointment in Frankfurt.' (In 1989 Philip missed the cut at the German Open in the last qualifying event to rule out any chance he had of booking an automatic spot on the team.)

In 1995 Philip effectively secured his place on the team by beating Colin Montgomerie in a play-off for the English Open at the Forest of Arden in early June.

That victory moved him to seventh in the Ryder Cup table and prompted Montgomerie to say, 'He (Philip) was very brave out there today and I believe he would be a great asset in any Ryder Cup team.'

Even then Philip refused to talk about qualifying for the Ryder Cup. It proved to be a wise decision. He still had to get across the finishing line, and by the time the German Open came around in late August he had slipped to tenth and final place in the points table.

The Dubliner went into the last qualifying competition looking over his shoulder at Darren Clarke, Ian Woosnam and Sven Struver who were all capable of overtaking him. Making the cut was the first priority and he started well, opening with rounds of 68 and 69 to comfortably avoid the first hurdle. Now all he had to do was play steadily over the final two days to keep Clarke and Woosnam at arm's length.

A third round 71 set him up for a relaxed Sunday, and when he played the opening nine holes in 35 shots his selection seemed a formality. Then, suddenly, things started to spiral out of control. He played the final nine holes in 42 shots and slipped down the leaderboard at an alarming rate.

Philip Walton celebrates Europe's Ryder Cup victory over America at Oak Hill (September 1995).

Philip Walton (*extreme left*) **with the victorious European Ryder Cup team (September 1995).**

His final round 77 eventually left him in a tie for eighth last place and he earned a paltry 968 Ryder Cup points.

Thankfully, it didn't turn out to be too costly, with Clarke and Woosnam both failing to do enough to shift him from tenth place. It was, however, a worrying collapse and one that once again raised fears about his ability to handle pressure.

'When it came down to the nitty-gritty my mind was just not there,' he admitted honestly. 'The last six weeks have been a nightmare, but it's over now and I feel I deserve my place in the team.'

It was, in his own words, 'a weird way to finish', but Philip received immediate support from European captain Bernard Gallacher.

'Philip has had a tough last few weeks and he is obviously very relieved to have made the team,' said Gallacher. 'He has been under a lot of strain, but he's a very good player and a straight driver, which will be a considerable asset at Oak Hill.'

Philip's inclusion in the 1995 Ryder Cup team was a victory for perseverance in the face of adversity. Always a talented ball-striker, he turned professional in 1983 after two Walker Cup appearances in 1981 and 83.

His problems lay on the greens and it wasn't until he turned to the broom-handle putter in late 1993 that he finally became a force to be reckoned with. Before that he was little more than a journeyman pro, but one who still managed to make a decent living for his family, wife Suzanne and children Hayley and Rhys (the Waltons would have a third child Sian in 1996).

His one tour victory before his double success in 1995 came in the Peugeot Open de France in 1990. Instead of progressing after that first win, Philip had struggled badly in the early 90s finishing well down the European money ladder, which left him with serious doubts about his game.

Switching to the broom-handle putter gave him a lifeline which he grabbed with both hands. 'The long putter has been the making of him,' said David Feherty. 'He was always a beautiful striker of the ball. He just struck it too often when he got on the green, that's all.'

'Philip has had a tough last few weeks and he is obviously very relieved to have made the team.'

Wielding his new putter to great effect, Philip gradually regained his confidence which gave him the self-belief to target a Ryder Cup place as the 1995 season got under way.

By earning his right to play in the 1995 Ryder Cup, Philip completed a remarkable clean sweep of amateur and professional team honours. He played amateur golf for Ireland, played in the Walker Cups in 1981 and 83, winning six points out of a possible eight, and he was also a member of the British and Irish team that competed in the Eisenhower Trophy in 1982.

In the professional ranks he was a member of the Irish side that won the Dunhill Cup for a second time in 1990 and by the time the Ryder Cup got under way, he and Darren Clarke had been confirmed as Ireland's representatives at the World Cup.

Question marks remained about his ability to handle the peculiar stresses of the Ryder Cup, but in general the Irish press felt that Philip had the game to succeed at Oak Hill. They pointed to his superb team record,

particularly in the Walker Cup, as evidence that he not only deserved to be on the plane to America, but would also be a valuable member of Bernard Gallacher's team.

This was Gallacher's third and final appearance as Europe's Ryder Cup captain and he desperately wanted to sign off on a winning note following narrow defeats in 1991 and 93. The Scot was once again relying on the same players who had piloted Europe to Ryder Cup victories in the late 80s.

With Faldo, Ballesteros (whose powers were on the wane), Langer and Woosnam (a late replacement for the injured José Maria Olazabal) in his side, he had plenty of experience to call on, but there was a feeling, certainly among the American press, that many of the Europeans were clinging on to past glories. Just two rookies made the team, Philip Walton and Sweden's Per-Ulrik Johansson.

Gallacher's watchword before the event got under way was 'flexibility'. He fully understood that some of his team were not in great form going into the matches and that with seven players over 37 years of age there could be issues of fatigue. However, he remained positive and as practice began he spoke of Europe's need to improve their performance in the final day singles if they were to upset the odds and win on American soil.

'Our record in the singles isn't good and it's something I intend to discuss with the players. It comes down to attitude. I see no reason why we shouldn't win the singles, but we need to be in the right frame of mind,' he said.

The Americans were captained by Lanny Wadkins, a renowned match play competitor who had a fantastic Ryder Cup record. He had five rookies to contend with: Brad Faxon, Tom Lehman, Jeff Maggert, Phil Mickelson and Loren Roberts.

Similar to previous US captains, he was forced to turn to experience with his wildcard picks and selected Fred Couples (who had a moderate Ryder Cup record) and, more controversially, Curtis Strange (who hadn't won a PGA tournament in six years). Wadkins, however, refused to admit that the American qualification system had dealt him a poor hand.

'Our way of doing things (over two years instead of one like Europe) means that I have players who have been performing consistently week in, week out,' he said. 'As far as I'm concerned, our system ensures that instead of streaky players, I've got 12 guys who are playing good, solid, competitive golf.'

The one thing Wadkins could control was the set-up of Oak Hill, and the Europeans were confronted with a course with thick, heavy rough, narrow fairways and slick greens. Wadkins wanted it to look and feel like

clubs went missing in transit, he saw nothing to be frightened about.

'I love it. It's a superb course, one of the finest I've seen, and I think I can play really well here,' he said. 'Naturally, with all the oak trees around it's tight, particularly off the tee. But straight driving is one of the strengths of my game.'

Practice went well and Philip declared himself pleased with how he was settling in. Partnering Sam Torrance on the final practice day, he expressed his belief that they would make a decent pairing, not least because they both used broom-handle putters.

'My game is about 90 per cent right at the moment,' added Philip. 'I have got a little bit of work to do around the greens. I just have to get a little bit of education on the shots around the green.'

Despite showing up well in practice, Philip was left out of the opening foursomes along with Ian Woosnam and, more surprisingly, Seve Ballesteros. Gallacher was forced to defend his omission of Ballesteros explaining, 'I'm trying to put what we consider to be the best

> 'I love it. It's a superb course, one of the finest I've seen, and I think I can play really well here.'

the course had been set up to host a US Open, and he got his wish.

'The key is keeping the ball out of the rough,' he said. 'Since I get to decide how much rough there'll be, I can tell you there will be plenty.'

Not that this bothered Philip too much as he immediately took a shine to Oak Hill. Forced to walk the course on Monday instead of practising after his

foursomes players on the course. It's not a gamble. Seve's game is about bogeys and birdies, and foursomes play isn't about that.'

There was nothing for Philip to do but continue practising, and this he did diligently as he waited for the nod from Gallacher. He was also left out of the afternoon fourballs on day one and was clearly wondering if he would be left on the sidelines until Sunday when Gallacher confirmed that he would

Philip Walton is embraced by team mate Per-Ulrik Johansson (September 1995).

The Europeans as a whole were certainly 'keyed up and ready to go' as the foursomes got under way. Sam Torrance and Costantino Rocca hammered Davis Love and Jeff Maggert 6 and 5, and there were also big victories for Montgomerie and Faldo and Langer and Gilford.

Philip and Ian Woosnam found themselves in a tight battle with Loren Roberts and Peter Jacobsen.

The Europeans led by two after the opening four holes before an American birdie on the

Philip Walton (*nearest the camera*) **is ferried back to the club house during the Murphy's Irish Open at Ballybunion, Co. Kerry (June 2000).**

partner Ian Woosnam in the morning foursomes on day two.

It came as the Scot admitted he had made a mistake in keeping the Bernhard Langer/Per-Ulrik Johansson pairing involved in the afternoon fourballs on day one. Europe trailed 5-3 at the end of day one and Gallacher held up his hands admitting that he was partly to blame.

'My error was not anticipating a long match and the fact that they (Langer and Johansson) would only have a break of half an hour,' he said. 'I realise now that I should have gone for Philip and Ian. It was a mistake.'

Philip was understandably relieved to be finally getting a chance to play. It had been a frustrating wait but he was determined to make the most of his chance.

'It had got to the stage that I didn't know whether I would play before Sunday or not. So I'm obviously delighted. Woosie and I will do well together. We're keyed up and ready to go,' he said.

5th cut the deficit to one. At the par three 6th Philip rattled in a 25 foot putt to regain the two-hole lead, but it was soon wiped out and at the turn the sides were level.

Woosnam rammed home a birdie putt at the 11th to put Europe in front again, but the Americans hit back with birdies at the 12th and 13th to take the lead for the first time in the match.

A European bogey at the 14th left them two behind before Woosnam holed another putt of 20 feet on the 15th to cut the deficit to one. On the 16th Philip missed a six-footer which would have levelled the sides, and with the 17th halved in par the Europeans started up the 18th trailing by one.

The pressure was now firmly on Roberts and Jacobsen. The American team desperately needed something from the match and somehow they managed to get up and down from 90 yards to par the last and record a one-hole victory.

'Neither Philip nor Ian played at their very best and they didn't seem to gel, although they got a lot out of their match and encouraged each other,' said Philip's caddie Bryan McLauchlan.

'We could still have easily got a half out of it, but we didn't. Perhaps if we had, things might have turned out completely differently. It was all fate that week.'

A 3-1 victory in the morning foursomes left the sides level at six wins each heading into what looked like a vital session of fourballs. The perceived wisdom was that Europe needed to come out of the afternoon with an overall lead.

Gallacher juggled his pairings for the afternoon and Philip missed out again. Woosnam, however, partnered Rocca to victory over Davis Love and Ben Crenshaw.

It was the only victory in a depressing afternoon for Europe, capped by American Corey Pavin chipping

He was almost right. After Seve lost to Tom Lehman at the top of the singles, his middle order picked up six and a half points, but that still left Europe needing a full point from either Philip or Johansson.

When Johansson lost 3 and 2 to Phil Mickelson, the result hinged on the man from Malahide and he didn't disappoint, clinging on for that famous gut-wrenching one-hole win over Haas.

'I can't believe it. It's the biggest day of my life,' said Philip, moments after holing the winning putt.

'The pressure is unbelievable. I've never experienced anything quite like it. But I always felt sure we could do it. In fact, before we left Dublin I bet £1,000 on Europe at 5-2. I can't believe it all came down to me.'

It was an emotional finale but the reception he and the rest of the European team received 24 hours later when Concorde touched down at Dublin Airport was simply

> 'I can't believe it. It's the biggest day of my life,' said Philip, moments after holing the winning putt.

in on the 18th to beat Faldo and Langer. America had regained the two-point cushion they had at the start of the day, and leading 9-7 the pundits predicted a third consecutive victory for the US. It would all come down to the final day and Gallacher's earlier statement about winning the singles would now be put to the test.

He gambled when naming his singles order, putting a misfiring Seve out first, 'because he couldn't lose the Ryder Cup from that position', and then packed the middle of the order with his strongest players. He put his two rookies in at the end in the hope that the outcome of the match would not come down to either of them.

unforgettable. Some 3,000 fans gathered in the rain to greet the team and Philip had the honour of carrying the trophy off the plane and into the terminal.

'I know we pulled off a great success, but this is just spectacular,' said Philip. 'It has been an intense week. Nothing can prepare you for the pressures of playing in a Ryder Cup, absolutely nothing. I've never experienced anything like that period from the 18th tee to the green, but I will remember it forever.'

Chapter 15

Darren Clarke

Darren Clarke plays a shot to the 1st green during the Ryder Cup at the Belfry (September 2002).

For a split second Darren Clarke must have thought he was back at Brookline, scene of Europe's final day collapse in 1999.

He had made the mistake of looking at one of the leaderboards and all he could see was a rash of red numbers. The roars of the crowd at Oakland Hills (Ryder Cup 2004) confirmed his worst fears — the Americans were making a final day charge. 'Looking at the board early, with all the red up there, was not a great sight for us,' he said later. 'We're always told don't look at the board, but you can't help yourself. You've got to look now and again to see what's going on.'

In 2002 at the Belfry it had all been so different. Leading from the front, Colin Montgomerie had ensured Europe got off to a blistering start in the final day singles. 'There was a lot of blue. So it's always good to see that. It gives you a little bit of impetus,' said Darren.

At Oakland Hills, the impetus was clearly with the Americans, but Darren was confident there would be no repeat of Brookline. Instead of being swept away, the European players turned the tide and by the end of the day they had inflicted their heaviest defeat on a US team, winning 18½-9½.

'You know, we as 12 team members have great confidence in each other, and we had a chat last night about everybody playing for their own point as if he was playing for the Ryder Cup,' Darren told the assembled media.

'Everybody kept on going and we managed to reverse a lot of those red numbers this afternoon. That's the way

Darren Clarke *(right)* **and Lee Westwood celebrate a Ryder Cup foursomes victory over Tiger Woods and Phil Mickelson at Oakland Hills Country Club, Michigan, USA (September 2004).**

we have been all week. No matter what was going on, the other guys are going to pull for each other. That's why at the end of the week we have ended up with as many points as we have.'

Victory at Oakland Hills meant a hell of a lot to Darren. For him the Ryder Cup is all about pride: in one's own performance, in the team, in the European Tour, and in Ireland's strong heritage with the event.

'If you look at the guys that have done well: Paul McGinley, Philip Walton, Eamonn Darcy holing out at Muirfield Village, Christy O'Connor — it just seems to keep coming down to the Irish guys,' he said. 'It's a great little piece of history to be part of and be proud of.'

The manner of Europe's capitulation at Brookline in 1999 had left a sour taste which Darren had never fully got rid of, in spite of Europe's victory at the Belfry in 2002. He needed to beat the Americans in their own backyard and Europe's sweeping success at Oakland Hills tasted very sweet indeed.

'I think people didn't expect us to perform so well, and unfortunately for the US guys we played very, very well,' he said.

● ● ● ●

It's almost impossible to think of a European team without Darren Clarke at its very heart. Born in 1968 in Dungannon, Co. Tyrone, Darren has now competed in four Ryder Cups and has become increasingly influential in the European cause.

Married to Heather and with two sons, Tyrone and Conor, he is recognised as something of a match play expert.

He started taking golf seriously as an 11 year old at Dungannon Golf Club and was playing off scratch within a couple of years. His aggressive shot-making ability was ideally suited to the one-on-one form of the game, and it quickly drew him to the attention of the Irish and Ulster selectors. His love of match play developed through his participation at boys, youths and senior level in the amateur game.

> **'Everybody kept on going and we managed to reverse a lot of those red numbers this afternoon.'**

'I don't think we did anything wrong at Brookline. We certainly were not complacent (Europe went into the singles with a four-point lead),' said Darren. 'We knew we still had a job to do, but we went out and didn't play well enough. The Americans simply played better than we did.'

It was a completely different story at Oakland Hills, with the Europeans dominating from the start and maintaining a stranglehold on proceedings throughout the three days.

'I grew up playing a lot of match play,' he said. 'You can take on shots you wouldn't in a normal tournament. You can afford to gamble. That's what makes it more exciting.'

Darren was a prolific winner on the amateur circuit. In 1990, the year he turned professional, he beat Paul McGinley by one hole to win the North of Ireland title. In the same year he also picked up the South of Ireland crown and the Irish Amateur Close Championship, beating Padraig Harrington 3 & 2 at Baltray.

A Walker Cup place was his for the taking, but he took the plunge and joined the professional ranks. After a couple of lean years, he made his professional breakthrough in 1993, winning the Alfred Dunhill Open at Royal Zoute Golf Club in Belgium with a two-shot victory over Nick Faldo.

Since that first win, Darren has developed into a truly global player, contending in majors (he finished second in the 1997 Open Championship) and winning around the world.

His prowess as a match play competitor was underlined in 2000 when he won the WGC Accenture Match Play Championship at La Costa Resort and Spa. The victory netted him a cool $1 million. In the process he beat David Duval in the semifinal before polishing off Tiger Woods in the 36-hole final.

He has ensured that he is an indispensable member of any European Ryder Cup challenge, and his value to the team is such that he has played every session of the last three Ryder Cups.

In all he has played 17 matches, winning seven but, surprisingly, he is still searching for his first singles victory. Not that individual success worries him. Darren may be a big character and one of the most recognised golfers in the world, but when it comes to the Ryder Cup he thinks only of doing his bit to help the European cause.

Darren Clarke hits a drive during the Ryder Cup at Oakland Hills (September 2004).

Darren Clarke in action during the Ryder Cup at Brookline Country Club, Boston, USA (September 1999).

'We are all pulling for the guy to make the four-footer coming down the stretch on Sunday,' he said at Oakland Hills.

'It would not be quite the same against him, but we all want to help each other as much as we possibly can.

The bond we get with the fellow players this week is like nothing else, because week in, week out you're trying to beat the same guys you are now pulling for.

'To have guys like Paul McGinley holing the putt at the Belfry, Monty against Scott Hoch at Valderrama — you

When it comes to the Ryder Cup he thinks only of doing his bit to help the European cause.

Darren Clarke *(left)* **in relaxed mood during the Ryder Cup at the Belfry. American player Tiger Woods is pictured in the background (September 2002).**

know, being part of that team is something we don't experience. So whenever you do experience it and we are part of the winning team, it is very, very special.'

He is also aware of how vital the Ryder Cup is for the future of the European Tour. 'In Europe we have made huge leaps and bounds in the past six, seven years, where prize funds are going up and courses are getting better,' he said.

'For us the extra interest we generate through winning the Ryder Cup means a lot to the tour and helps us

'For us the extra interest we generate through winning the Ryder Cup means a lot to the tour.'

grow and get bigger. So from that point of view, I think it is more important for us as Europeans to win it in terms of the European Tour, than the PGA Tour.'

Darren made his Ryder Cup debut at Valderrama in 1997 under the captaincy of Seve Ballesteros. It proved to be a frustrating time as Ballesteros left him out altogether on the opening day.

'I didn't have a relationship with Seve at all. He spoke about five words to me all week,' said Darren. 'I couldn't understand why I wasn't playing on the first day. I had qualified second on the team. I hadn't just

scraped in. That's his decision to make, of course. Seve is a legend.'

Darren was eventually let off the leash in the opening fourball match on day two, partnering Colin Montgomerie against Davis Love and Fred Couples.

'I remember teeing the ball up on the 1st tee and I made sure I teed it up a little bit higher to just hope that I made contact with it on the way down,' said Darren. 'Unfortunately, I veered a little bit too far to the left, but I managed to find it.'

Tiger Woods *(left)* **and Darren Clarke share a joke during the Ryder Cup at Oakland Hills (September 2004).**

Darren Clarke plays from a bunker during the afternoon foursomes at the Belfry (September 2002).

The Americans led by two at the 10th but at the 11th Darren holed a birdie putt to cut the deficit, and Montgomerie brought the sides level by holing a five-footer on the 12th. The Europeans won the 17th to take a vital one-hole lead, and a par at the 18th was good enough to secure a first Ryder Cup point for Darren.

Driven along by Seve's promptings, the Europeans won a further five points on day two at Valderrama and took a five-point lead into the final day.

Darren faced Phil Mickelson in the singles and was three down after four holes, courtesy of a birdie-birdie-eagle blitz from the American. He fought back, birdied the 9th and was just one down as they went to the 11th.

In the rough on the par five 11th, Mickelson somehow conjured up a bit of magic and chipped in for his second eagle of the round to go two up. The American gave Darren a hole back at the 14th, but he stayed in control and birdies on the 16th and 17th gave him a 2 and 1 win.

'He had two incredible eagles on the par fives and he got up and down from impossible places a few times as well,' said Darren. 'It's tough to win holes when your opponent's short game is as sharp as his was.'

Valderrama proved to be something of an unfulfilling experience for Darren. He was part of a winning side as Europe just about hung on for victory, but he had been a peripheral figure, a role he wasn't comfortable playing. He couldn't help the team sitting on the sidelines. He needed to be in the thick of the action.

When Mark James took over the captaincy ahead of the 1999 Ryder Cup at Brookline, he understood how crucial it was to have Darren more involved in the proceedings.

The old guard, Faldo, Langer and Woosnam, had all failed to qualify and his team looked short of experience as they flew out to America. James realised that to have any chance of success he needed his big-

Members of the same management stable and close friends off the golf course, theirs is a natural pairing. When it comes to matters golfing, there are few people Darren Clarke trusts more than Westwood.

'Lee and I have travelled around the world and played together many, many times,' said Darren.

'Whenever we're playing in foursomes, I don't care where he hits it and he doesn't care where I hit it because we both have trust in each other's ability. That makes it an awful lot easier when you are not worried about where you are hitting for your partner.'

> ## 'Lee and I have travelled around the world and played together many, many times.'

name players like Clarke and Lee Westwood playing to their full potential, and he felt that an all-embracing team ethic would help to get the best out of his men.

'I knew it would be a big help to him (Clarke) if we had a good team atmosphere with everybody happy and enjoying the week', wrote James in *Into the Bear Pit*.

'If that happened, then I was sure Darren would be ready to play. When he is tuned in, it is difficult to think of anything he does not do well because he has a huge talent, hits the ball long and straight, can go high or low with his irons and has a very good putting stroke.'

It was with those thoughts in mind that James also launched the Clarke/Westwood partnership on an unsuspecting American public. Since 1999, the two men have played six times together for Europe, winning four matches and claiming some notable scalps along the way.

They played four times together at Brookline, emerging with a 50 per cent record and a prized victory over the American Nos 1 and 2, Tiger Woods and David Duval. Darren has fond memories of that fourball match on the opening day of competition at Brookline, and not just because they ended up with a one-hole victory.

'It was the most fun I've ever had on the golf course,' he said later. 'We chatted all the way round. We were trying to win but that side of things can get lost. We had a great time telling jokes, all sorts of stuff, and that's the spirit in which I think the Ryder Cup should be played.'

Brookline ultimately finished on a sour note for the Europeans. Their four-point lead was gobbled up early on the final day, and the Americans rammed home their superiority in the singles, winning 8½ points out of the 12 on offer.

Darren, who had volunteered to go out second behind Westwood, chipped in to win the opening hole in his match with Hal Sutton, but the American responded, winning the next three holes on the bounce and from there he never looked back, eventually winning 4 and 2.

'We were hoping that Lee or I would get a point from the first two games,' said Darren. 'But it went wrong. Tom Lehman (who played Westwood) and Hal Sutton simply played better than us. How good the Americans played in the singles was very much overlooked amid all the furore at the end.'

The 'furore' involved the manner of America's victory at Brookline. The crowd, fuelled by patriotic fervour, got out of hand and the atmosphere turned decidedly nasty for the Europeans. Darren diplomatically described it as 'electrifying', but the American players certainly fed off it, encouraged it and got carried away.

When Justin Leonard holed a massive putt on the 17th green in his match with José Maria Olazabal, it sparked a mass invasion, even though Olazabal still

actually get that every week. We are here to provide entertainment for the fans of golf.'

In fact, Darren has often spoken about how difficult it can be playing against friends in the Ryder Cup — the sense of wanting to play well and win but at the same time hoping your opponent also performs well.

The postponement of the Ryder Cup gave everybody an extra year to consider how they would approach the event. It also gave the captains an extra year to worry about getting the best out of their respective teams.

European captain Sam Torrance knew from the start that he would eventually end up with the core of the team who played at Brookline and for that reason he knew motivation was never going to be a problem. However, the extra year was not kind to him.

He had quite an inexperienced line-up and many of his players had lost form and confidence over the

> # Darren has often spoken about how difficult it can be playing against friends in the Ryder Cup.

had a putt for a half (which he eventually missed). The recriminations continued for many months, and the sense of injustice felt by Europe looked certain to overshadow the 2001 Ryder Cup at the Belfry.

It took the terrorist attacks on the World Trade Center in 2001 to make people realise that the Ryder Cup was not life or death. That realisation came as a great relief to Darren who hankered for a return to a more innocent time of friendly competition.

'The Ryder Cup is supposed to be a spectator spectacle and they get to see some of the best players in the world go head-to-head with each other,' he said. 'We don't

intervening 12 months. That included Lee Westwood who had plummeted down the world rankings since Brookline. Torrance made the decision early that he would have to split the Clarke/Westwood partnership. He opted instead to pair Darren with Denmark's Thomas Bjorn.

The new pairing settled down quickly in practice and Torrance threw them into the deep end by letting them lead the way for Europe against Tiger Woods and Paul Azinger in the opening fourball on Friday morning. It proved to be an inspired decision by Torrance, with Bjorn holing a 15-footer on the last to win one up.

European team members Miguel Angel Jimenez *(left)* and Darren Clarke *(right)* celebrate their fourball victory over America's Davis Love III and Chad Campbell (September 2004).

'There's nothing quite like Friday morning,' said Darren. 'The atmosphere at the Belfry — you could cut it with a knife. It was very nerve-racking, but as soon as we got off the 1st tee it was fine.'

Europe got off to a winning start but the Bjorn/Clarke partnership failed to find the winners' circle in two subsequent outings and Torrance split them on Saturday afternoon, pairing Darren with cup rookie Paul McGinley in the final fourball of the day.

In a fluctuating encounter, the Irishmen were two down to Scott Hoch and Jim Furyk at the 13th, all square after 16, and then one down again playing the

18th hole. Europe desperately needed a half to go into the singles all square, and McGinley came through, winning the hole to give Europe a fighting chance which they made the most of by winning the final day singles 7½-4½.

Darren, playing third behind Colin Montgomerie and Sergio Garcia, had a nip and tuck singles match with David Duval which eventually saw both men get up and down for pars on the 18th and a deserved half.

Two years later at Oakland Hills, Darren had a golden opportunity to break his singles duck against Davis Love III. Trailing for most of the match, he won the 16th

Lee Westwood and Darren Clarke celebrate during the Ryder Cup at Brookline (September 1999).

and then fashioned a superb chip-in birdie on the 17th to level things as the players headed down the 18th. Love was in trouble off the tee and could do no better than a five, leaving Darren with a four foot putt for victory, which somehow lipped out.

'Davis and I are very good friends. You know, on 18 I wanted to say "good/good" (both players concede putts for a half),' said Darren.

'If I had seen the scoreboard I definitely would have picked his ball up and said "good/good" because the way our game went it deserved to be a half and no other result. He's disappointed with his putt on the 18th green and so am I, but a half was a fair result for both of us.'

Darren enjoyed his best Ryder Cup return at Oakland Hills, claiming 3½ points as Europe hammered the US.

The Clarke/Westwood partnership made a triumphant reappearance in the foursomes on day one against the top American pairing of Tiger Woods and Phil Mickelson.

Taking on the best that the US has to offer is always guaranteed to provoke an inspired display from both Clarke and Westwood, and they rose to the occasion. If anything, this was a better victory than the one over Duval and Woods in 1999,

they then won the 10th and the 11th to go ahead for the first time. The Americans won the 17th with a par to draw level, but then a wild tee-shot by Mickelson effectively handed the point to Europe.

'You know, the two of us, we can play now and again and we're not easily intimidated by anyone,' said Darren later to the media.

'We looked upon today as an opportunity for the two of us to go out and not so much prove ourselves but to enjoy ourselves and take on the No. 2 and No. 4 in the world.

> ## 'If I had seen the scoreboard I definitely would have picked his ball up and said "good".'

with the European pairing showing the value of experience to come back from three down after four holes, winning with a par on the 18th.

'Going out against Tiger and Phil, we were both really looking forward to it,' said Darren. 'We knew that they would want to come out firing to get some points on the board for the US. When they did get off to a good start, we just had to settle down and try to play our way back into the match, which we did.

'We just steadied the ship and kept on going. Having been in these situations before in Ryder Cup foursomes, we knew things can turn around very quickly.'

By the turn Darren and Lee were just one down and

'We managed to do that and just come through and get another point for the team. We're here, team members, but certainly that was a great point for us to turn the game around and come back and win that point.

'I holed a putt — I think it was on 14 — from about four to five feet for a half. I turned to Lee and said, "You know, we've come a long way from Valderrama."

'At Valderrama we were both rookies and now we know what we are doing an awful lot better. Hence after going three down we didn't panic. Whereas, if it had been our first Ryder Cup — (a) we would not have been playing, and (b) we definitely would have been panicking.'

Chapter 16

Padraig Harringt

Padraig Harrington in action at Oakland Hills (September 2004).

on

Mark James was terrified.

The crowd at Brookline was getting out of hand and Europe's four-point lead going into the singles had evaporated in the face of a remarkable American fight back. He needed the players at the bottom of the singles to come through with some points if Europe was going to retain the trophy.

His experienced men, Colin Montgomerie and José Maria Olazabal, seemed to be in control of their matches, but he still needed one of his debutants to come through and, in his estimation, Padraig Harrington was his best bet. The Irishman had impressed him all week. He had booked his place on the team at the last minute with second place finishes in the two final qualifying competitions, the West of Ireland Classic and the BMW International. As a consequence, he was confident coming into the event and he had managed to maintain his excellent form.

Padraig Harrington hits a drive during his Ryder Cup singles match with Jay Haas at Oakland Hills (September 2004).

The problem was that with his match against Mark O'Meara hanging in the balance, Padraig had just asked James what club he should hit at the par three 16th.

'I got this terrible sinking feeling as I walked across the tee because I knew he wanted to know what club to hit. My only thought was that this could be the first time a captain had ever mis-clubbed a player to lose the Ryder Cup', stated James in his book, *Into the Bear Pit.*

'It was not a nice feeling. I thought, my God, I'm going to be responsible for the whole thing right here. Padraig soon confirmed what I had suspected; he was between a smooth six-iron and a big seven.

'I had no idea what to advise, but finally opted for the suggestion that he would probably be better off with a

'I was aware of how important my match was, given the intensity surrounding it and the pressure the crowd was putting on Mark O'Meara,' said Padraig.

'The whole week was as good as I've ever been mentally, before and since. I was so focused on the Sunday. I never saw a leaderboard, I saw one person the whole day.

'I never saw my own team mates. I saw Mark James on the 16th, but besides that I'm told afterwards that guys were coming up trying to encourage me. I didn't hear anything, I didn't see anything.'

The two men traded holes over the opening nine, and by the 13th it was all square and it remained that way as they stood on the 18th tee.

After a perfect drive, and with O'Meara in a bunker,

'It was not a nice feeling. I thought, my God, I'm going to be responsible for the whole thing right here.'

smooth six because, whatever wind there was, it was slightly hurting.

'I retreated back to the bench, holding my breath, and only exhaled when he hit quite a good shot 25 feet left of the pin. It was the right club, but it had frightened the hell out of me thinking that I could have blown everything.'

It was unlikely that James's nervous response even registered with Padraig. He was entirely consumed with seeing off O'Meara.

Padraig readily admits that he has rarely managed to find the same focus that saw him through to victory that Sunday at Brookline.

Padraig was left with a short iron of 148 yards to the flag. When he got to his ball, he settled himself and hit what he later described as 'probably the best shot I hit all week' to around ten feet. With O'Meara unable to get up and down from a greenside bunker, the Dubliner two-putted for a superb victory.

'When I won the match it was very emotional, because I'd never allowed myself to get ahead of myself and think I was going to win the match,' he said.

● ● ● ●

Padraig Harrington never thought for one moment that he would one day spearhead Europe's challenge in the Ryder Cup.

The Dubliner, now a regular fixture in the world's top 20, had more modest ambitions when he embarked on a career in professional golf.

'I would have been delighted to become a journeyman pro on the tour,' he said. 'I started off and I was quite successful straight away, and I have just kept my head down and kept going since then.

'I really haven't looked around. If I sat and thought about it, I think I would struggle. When things are going well, you just have to keep going with it and not question.'

He did, of course, harbour dreams of playing in the event and is acutely aware of Ireland's special relationship with the Ryder Cup.

'My Ryder Cup recollections mainly stem around the Irish,' he said. 'Obviously I remember Sam Torrance's putt in 1985 and the win, but I was not that much into golf in 85. I was more into Gaelic football and

'The Irish guys have done exceptionally well. Christy O'Connor held the record and, to be honest, that's another memory. I used to play a lot of golf in Royal Dublin. The spike bar has ten photographs of Christy Snr on the walls. That is some heritage and I was very conscious of it when I was growing up playing golf.'

Padraig may not have harboured genuine ambitions to one day lead the way for Europe, but his rise to the top has not been based on good fortune. The 35 year old is one of the hardest working golfers in the world. His modest approach and genial air hides a driven and dedicated professional who continues to spend long hours honing his game.

Blessed with a wonderful short game that helped him to the top of the Irish amateur ranks and a place on the 1991, 93 and 95 Walker Cup teams, Padraig was realistic enough to admit that his ball-striking was simply not good enough for the professional game.

Since turning professional in 1995 he has remodelled

'I really haven't looked around. If I sat and thought about it, I think I would struggle.'

Irish sports. I would have been well into golf by 87. I remember Eamonn Darcy holing that putt at Muirfield, which I still think today is one of the best putts I've ever seen holed, especially knowing that for Eamonn it would not be his favourite putt, to hole a four or five-footer downhill that was going to go off the green if it missed. That was one of the earliest and biggest memories that I have.

'I can remember the rest of the Irish golfers, Christy O'Connor, Philip Walton holing the winning putt, Paul McGinley obviously; all of them have performed. David Feherty also performed well.

his swing under the guidance of Howard Bennett and then Bob Torrance, developing into a world-class player. He has won on both sides of the Atlantic, faced down Tiger Woods and contended in majors.

In the Ryder Cup he has played 12 matches, winning seven, losing four and halving one. More importantly, he has a 100 per cent singles record: played three, won three. Mind you, he is not sure if he actually 'enjoys' the event.

'I suppose it's like going on a roller coaster,' he said.

European team players Padraig Harrington *(left)* **and Paul McGinley celebrate their victory over Tiger Woods and Davis Love III at Oakland Hills (September 2004).**

'When you're actually on the roller coaster it's not much fun, but when you get off you think it's fun. It's the same with the Ryder Cup. The week after the event, I would never want to play in another one, but three months later I think I liked it and want to play another one.

'When you play in the Ryder Cup there's probably nothing as intense or as exciting for somebody like me to play in. I'd have to take up some weird sport in order to get that sort of adrenalin rush. It's great to that extent, but it's not enjoyable. Enjoyable is going to the movies.'

• • • •

Golf was a big part of Padraig's life growing up in Dublin. His father, Paddy, was involved in the development of Stackstown Golf Club in south County Dublin and, naturally, Padraig and his four brothers spent a lot of time there playing and practising.

It was a highly competitive sporting environment, with the five boys trying to outdo each other at all sports. While he enjoyed golf, it was seen as a game to be played during the holidays and was some way down the pecking order behind Gaelic games and soccer.

Padraig Harrington wills the ball into the hole on the final green of the Ryder Cup at the Belfry. The putt stayed out (September 2002).

It wasn't until he was 11 or 12 that he actually began to take golf more seriously. As he devoted more time to the game, Padraig's handicap gradually came down and at 15 he was playing off scratch and doing well enough on the amateur circuit to earn a call-up to the Irish Boys' team.

Over the next nine years Padraig, with his brother Tadhg caddying for him, established himself as a fixture on Irish teams from boys through youths and into the senior ranks.

In those early years his battling, gutsy displays marked him out as a specialist in the match play arena and a valuable member in the team environment, but he had to wait until 1994 before claiming his first 'major', beating Ken Kearney in the final of the West of Ireland Championship at County Sligo Golf Club.

He finished his amateur career in 1995 as a member of another Walker Cup squad and also claimed two further 'majors', the Irish Stroke Play and Irish Close Championship.

After completing his accountancy exams, Padraig headed off to the 1995 tour school and managed to earn his tour card at the first time of asking. The 24 year old moved seamlessly into the world of professional golf, making the cut in each of his first eight European Tour events of the 1996 season and then magically, in his tenth professional event, he won the Spanish Open.

The victory was built on a second round 64 at the Club de Campo in Madrid which put him in charge of the tournament and he never faltered, leading from the front to win by four strokes from Scotland's Gordon Brand Jnr. The victory announced Padraig as a genuine talent, but more importantly it granted him an exemption on tour, eased any money worries and convinced him that he could compete in the professional game.

From that moment, Padraig's career path has been one of continued progression. In 1997 he partnered Paul McGinley to victory in the World Cup in Kiawah Island, Ireland's first victory in the event since Christy O'Connor and Harry Bradshaw won in Mexico in 1958.

In early 2005, he bagged his first PGA Tour event in America, winning the Honda Classic at the Mirasol Country Club in Florida. In June he claimed his second PGA event, winning the Barclays Classic with an outrageous eagle putt on the last green.

By just 'keeping his head down and keeping going' he has booked a place among the world's golfing elite.

Married to Caroline in 1997 and with one son, Patrick, Padraig is now at a level where he is expected to compete for majors and win titles on a regular basis. Although he may not be entirely comfortable with it, his climb up the world rankings has marked him out as one of the key players on the European team.

At Brookline, Padraig got a crash course in the peculiar pressures and emotions that make the Ryder Cup so compelling for the players and supporters alike.

'I was on the greatest high when I won that match against Mark,' recalled Padraig. 'I did an interview that never made any sense; I probably didn't say anything

By just 'keeping his head down and keeping going' he has booked a place among the world's golfing elite.

Padraig Harrington plays from a bunker during practice ahead of the Ryder Cup at the Belfry (September 2002).

European players Colin Montgomerie *(left)* and Padraig Harrington share a joke during the Ryder Cup at the Belfry (September 2002).

in the interview and within five minutes I ran down the 18th fairway. I probably didn't run, I probably glided down to the 17th and sat down, and within 30 seconds of sitting down Justin Leonard holed that putt (the putt that secured victory for America) and it was

taken away. I went from the biggest high to the lowest low of my golfing career.'

He has been able to take the experience gained at Brookline into subsequent Ryder Cups, although at the

'I get on very well with Colin. I have a lot of respect for his game. Monty has the experience and I am usually pretty determined.'

Belfry in 2002 that knowledge counted for very little. Struggling with his game, Padraig managed an average return of two points from four matches.

The Ryder Cup puts huge pressure on the players and knocks them out of their normal routine and for someone like Padraig, who has a very methodical approach to his game, it can prove difficult to handle, particularly if your game is not quite on song.

'The funny thing with the Ryder Cup is that a certain amount of pressure stays throughout the whole week, even the practice rounds,' he said in an early press conference at the Belfry.

'Normally it comes and goes in tournaments. You only feel pressure on the last nine holes. But at the Ryder Cup it's there all week. That's why it's so intense.

'The Ryder Cup is the worst event in the world for preparation. It's not your own time, because you're in a match players', recalled Torrance in his autobiography.

'The Irishman turned out to be not the only team member in that particular boat. Omitting Harrington was tough, even though he asked to be rested in order to sort out his game.

'A player like Harrington can turn it on any time. But his game wasn't right and he needed a morning to sort himself out. In fact, he was on the range with my dad (Bob Torrance) until darkness while his team mates unwound in the team room with dinner and the usual banter.'

After giving Padraig the time he needed to work on his game, Torrance put him back into the fray on the

> 'The funny thing with the Ryder Cup is that a certain amount of pressure stays throughout the whole week, even the practice rounds.'

team. There's a lot to do. You hope to come into the Ryder Cup with everything ready to go but you have little time to practise, so you're just relaxing. Unfortunately, I feel like I do need to do some practice.'

After losing both matches on day one, captain Sam Torrance reluctantly left Padraig out of the morning foursomes on day two.

'I never thought at the start of the week that I would be leaving out Harrington, one of my definite five-

afternoon of day two partnering Colin Montgomerie in the fourballs. Montgomerie's steadying influence seemed to have the desired effect and the two men combined to beat Phil Mickelson and David Toms 2 and 1.

With his confidence restored, Padraig proceeded to hammer Mark Calcavecchia 5 and 4 in the Sunday singles as Europe claimed a stunning victory. He was never behind against Calcavecchia. He missed good chances to take the lead at the 1st and 2nd but finally

Padraig Harrington *(centre of picture with putter in hand)* **secures a Ryder Cup singles victory over Jay Haas on the 18th green at Oakland Hills (September 2004).**

went ahead at the 3rd and extended his lead to three after seven holes. On the 9th he hammered in a 50 foot putt to go four up and closed the match out with a birdie on the par three 14th.

'I've got to say, I wasn't a hundred per cent on top of my game this week. I had to focus and did the best with what I've got,' he stated in the aftermath of Europe's victory.

'When Mark gave me the opportunity, I took it. I had to have faith in what I was doing. I just had to get out there and do the best I could. Obviously when I got a few holes up, it was a question of keeping the pressure on.'

Two years later at Oakland Hills, Padraig was clearly a more complete player, but he was still trying to play down his growing role within the team.

'I just feel like I'm not a rookie. I feel like I'm right in the middle. I don't feel in any sense that I'm the leader going out on this team,' he said.

Padraig Harrington hits a shot from the fairway at Oakland Hills (September 2004).

'I don't feel I've sort of reached that stage yet. I don't see the other rookies — they are all my age, or I feel their age, though they are a bit younger than me — I don't feel they are looking up to me in that sense. No. Give me another ten years.'

Regardless of his public stance on his role within the team, Padraig accepted the responsibility of being Europe's highest ranked player coming into the event by partnering Colin Montgomerie in the opening fourball match at Oakland Hills. The pair actively sought to open proceedings on day one, guessing that they would face the American No. 1 and 2, Tiger Woods and Phil Mickelson.

'I get on very well with Colin. I have a lot of respect for his game,' he said. 'Monty has the experience and I am usually pretty determined.'

Both players knew that a victory for Europe in the top match would give the rest of the team a huge boost. It was a calculated risk, which paid off for them and Europe as they recorded a 2 and 1 victory.

'I have to say that myself and Colin were in a good frame of mind going out. We elected to play that match. That is what we expected and I suppose we wanted to put two solid guys in against them, two of our big hitters, let's say, and it worked,' said Padraig.

'I felt great on the 1st tee. This is my third Ryder Cup start and I went from not being able to see the ball, to not bad at the Belfry, and pretty good today. The only worry I had was putting the ball on the actual tee. After that, everything else was pretty solid.

'We definitely felt that it was going to be an important

match. We kind of felt it was worth more than a point, based on the fact that the US guys were expected to win. If we could put anything up against them and even stem the tide, get some blue figures up there, it would help the guys behind. That was the thinking in our team room. When we did get ahead and kept ahead, it definitely gave some momentum to the rest of the team.'

'We started off badly and Davis had played so well in the morning. We're playing Davis, we're playing Tiger, and I didn't really see a way out of it. Walking off the 2nd green Paul said, "let's play the golf course. Let's stop playing the two guys, let's concentrate on our own ball like it's a US Open and try to shoot under par."

'When we finished it off on 15 it was to get back to one

> # Out last, Padraig provided a fitting finale by holing a 30 foot putt on the 18th green to beat Jay Haas one up.

The Montgomerie/Harrington combination proved to be a solid pairing for captain Bernhard Langer as they combined to secure two points out of three matches.

Padraig actually beat Tiger Woods twice at Oakland Hills. Having seen him off partnering Montgomerie, he recorded a more remarkable victory in the company of fellow Dubliner Paul McGinley in the afternoon foursomes on day two.

The Irishmen started badly and were two down after two holes to Woods and Davis Love III, but they dragged themselves back into the match, and a regulation par at the par four 8th levelled things. From there the good friends took command and built a three-hole lead with pars on the 9th, 11th and 13th before Padraig closed the match out with a five foot birdie putt on the 15th.

The win meant that Europe took a six-point lead into the final day singles and owed much to the persuasive powers of McGinley, who had given his partner a pep-talk coming off the 2nd green.

'It was a tough game for me going out,' said Padraig. 'I was a bit flat from the morning. (He and Montgomerie had lost to Stewart Cink and Davis Love.) I had missed a few putts in the morning and was just a bit flat going out.

under for the round. You know, it was as Paul said, let's shoot under par, and it did the job.'

In front of a raucous bunch of Irish fans the two Dubliners ensured that Europe took a massive six-point lead into the final day singles. This time there was no sign of a Brookline-style recovery from the Americans as the inspired Europeans went on to record their largest margin of victory, winning 18½-9½.

Out last, Padraig provided a fitting finale by holing a 30 foot putt on the 18th green to beat Jay Haas one up.

'This is probably the greatest experience I've ever had on a golf course,' Padraig said as Europe celebrated. 'Brookline was the most intense, and you know, winning at the Belfry was just unbelievable because it had been so tight at Brookline.

'Brookline made the Belfry. This time around it's a little bit different. We played great and couldn't have expected anything like this. We were predicting a tight match all the way through the weekend. It was a surprise to win.'

Chapter 17

Paul McGinley

Paul McGinley flies the flag for Ireland after being dumped in the lake following his winning putt for Europe during the Ryder Cup at the Belfry (September 2002).

If Paul McGinley could bottle one moment of his golfing career it would be those few seconds before he hit the winning putt for Europe at the Belfry in 2002.

He had trailed America's Jim Furyk right from the start of his singles match, but he never buckled and as the pressure intensified and the importance of his match gradually became apparent, he rose to the challenge.

'I was feeding off the crowd,' said Paul. 'It's important not to ignore them, but instead to use their emotion. It makes me drive forward; it doesn't make me back off. How can you when you have such vocal support behind you?'

Paul McGinley celebrates his putt on the 18th green which secured the Ryder Cup for Europe at the Belfry (September 2002).

Roared on by the fans and loving every minute of it, he cut the deficit to one hole and then bagged a 12-footer for birdie on the 17th to leave the match all square with one to play.

As the two players made their way on to the 18th green, European captain Sam Torrance spelt the situation out: if Paul could get down in two from the left of the green, Europe would win the Ryder Cup. When Furyk narrowly missed holing his bunker shot, the Dubliner was left with a testing 10 foot putt for glory.

'I was so completely in the present that I didn't consider any of the negative thoughts that were floating around in my head,' he said. 'I knew exactly how important the putt was, but I never dwelt on the prospect of missing. I got so involved in the process of putting, working out

himself,' said Paul.

'He said, "You know, me and you have something very important in common with each other."

'I said, what's that?

'He says, "We're both going to be remembered for putts: me for missing and you for holing."

'And I thought, wow, that's very big of him to say something like that. That's one of the things I'll always remember.'

Sanders may have been right about him being forever associated with that winning putt, but one appearance was never going to be enough for Paul. He needed to

"We're both going to be remembered for putts: me for missing and you for holing."

the line, getting the weight right and focusing on my routine, that it kept me right in the present.'

Looking remarkably calm and composed, Paul stepped up to the ball and almost casually rolled it into the hole to book himself a place in golfing history.

● ● ● ●

Three months after holing 'that putt', Paul McGinley was at a sports awards ceremony in Dublin when he was approached by the guest of honour, Doug Sanders. Sanders, a winner of 20 titles on the USPGA Tour, famously missed a 30 inch putt which would have won him the 1970 Open Championship.

'I had never met Doug before but as we were waiting to go in for dinner he came into the bar and introduced

be part of the 2004 team which defended the trophy at Oakland Hills in Detroit.

'People want to talk about that putt very regularly and that's okay,' he said. 'I feel blessed that it happened to me and it was a wonderful occasion and I will talk about it forever. But I want it to be part of my career as opposed to being the defining moment of my career.'

Publicly expressing his desire to make the team again, Paul shook off the effects of a mid-season knee injury and, ignoring the burden of expectation he had heaped upon himself, embarked on a gruelling ten-week playing schedule which culminated in his appearance at the final qualifying event, the BMW International in Munich.

With places on the team still up for grabs, he fashioned

four solid rounds, including a final day 68 in the company of Ryder Cup rival Fredrik Jacobsen to book his seat on the flight to America.

'It meant more to me to make that team. It was a harder team to get into,' he said. 'You look at all the guys that were doing their best to make it. There were five or six guys in the hunt for a captain's pick and all of them were worthy of making that side.'

The Ryder Cup has been very good to Paul McGinley, but then McGinley has been very good for the Ryder Cup. He is a committed European and a staunch supporter of the European Tour. He has played on two Ryder Cup teams and has come out on the winning side on both occasions.

That's not a bad return for someone who turned to golf relatively late in life. As a youngster, Paul's first

was tumbling and the realisation gradually dawned on him that he had a genuine aptitude for the game.

'I had just finished university (he completed a diploma in marketing) and had been working for a year or so when I thought to myself, maybe I could kill two birds with the one stone. I could go and do a couple of years in America by combining it with a scholarship,' said Paul.

He applied successfully to San Diego University, but his game simply wasn't strong enough at the time to secure a scholarship. Undeterred, he took out a bank loan, got some help from the Government and paid his way through what proved to be something of a 'finishing school'.

'Before going to America my expectations were that I might make the Walker Cup team as a good amateur,'

> # The Ryder Cup has been very good to Paul McGinley, but then McGinley has been very good for the Ryder Cup.

love was Gaelic football. Golf was a holiday sport, something to do while he waited for the next game of football or hurling. His father Mick, a member of Naas (outside Dublin), introduced him to golf at an early age, but by his own admission he had 'no interest in the game'.

It's likely that Irish golf would probably have lost Paul McGinley had he not picked up a knee injury which brought a premature end to his footballing career. The 19 year old was forced to find a new vehicle for his competitive instincts and golf provided the ideal outlet.

A year after putting his boots away and with a first season of winter golf under his belt, Paul's handicap

he said. 'By playing golf almost non-stop for two years, I turned from being a raw amateur who wasn't even in the Irish team, to coming back as the No. 1 Irish amateur.'

By the time Paul returned from America he had completed his degree and played on the 1991 GB & I Walker Cup team at Portmarnock partnering Liam White to a famous victory over Americans Phil Mickelson and Bob May. The 25 year old was at a crossroads. He could build a career in marketing, or he could try his hand at full-time golf.

With the positive experiences of the Walker Cup fresh in his mind, he made his way to the European Tour qualifying school and claimed a card at the first time of asking.

'When I went on tour first my mind was still wide open about how long I would be on tour, or what I would achieve,' added Paul. 'I wasn't a top player when I came out on tour, but I was good enough to survive. It was only after four or five years that I realised my game was coming round and that making the Ryder Cup was a realistic goal.

'I had always been aware of the Ryder Cup and the history of Irish golfers in the event. I wanted to be part of it, but I was never sure if I could reach those heights.

'Seve was the one I always looked out for. He was the one that stood out for me, and then all the Irish guys, the likes of Christy Jnr, Darce, Des, Rafferty. I always had an interest in anybody Irish. I still do. Any kind of Irish sports person doing well, and I will be pushing hard for them to succeed.'

It took Paul five years to find his feet on the European Tour and he broke his tournament duck with a victory in Austria at the Hohe Brucke Open in 1996, the same year he married his wife Alison. In 1997 he won the Oki Pro-Am in Madrid and later that year he partnered Padraig Harrington to a famous success in the World

Paul McGinley is mobbed by team mates after holing the winning putt at the Belfry (September 2002).

Paul McGinley holds aloft the Ryder Cup with his team mates in the background, including Padraig Harrington *(third from left)* **(September 2002).**

Cup at Kiawah Island. Firmly ensconced as one of the most consistent players on tour, Paul set his sights on making the 1999 Ryder Cup team but came up short, finishing outside the top ten.

'I realised at that stage that I was going to have to prepare properly and really give it a go if I wanted to be in the team for 2001 at the Belfry,' he added.

He eventually booked his berth on the team with room to spare, but his place wasn't guaranteed until he won a five-hole play-off for the rain-affected Celtic Manor Resort Wales Open title in early August 2001.

'It was a huge difference between first and second place in terms of Ryder Cup points, and that was really a lot of pressure and that's what drove me on,' he said,

moments after winning the title at Celtic Manor.

'It was on my mind. I would be lying if I said it wasn't. Since the Ryder Cup points list started, I felt I could make the team. I've been under the microscope and everybody was looking to see how I was doing, and there's been a lot of pressure on myself.'

That crucial victory came after two previous play-off defeats and highlighted his ability to come through when the pressure was at its most intense, a quality he later came to rely on in the Ryder Cup.

Paul was ranked 35th in the world and gearing up for his cup debut when the 11 September terrorist attacks on the World Trade Center in New York forced the event to be postponed for a year. The intervening period was not kind to his game and, shorn of focus, he slowly lost form and slipped out of the world's top 50. By the time the event got under way in September 2002, his game was off and he was ranked 65th in the world.

Bitterly disappointed with his performances, Paul admitted to the press that his poor displays had been playing on his mind.

'Everybody's form is going to go up and down over that period of time, and I think I have suffered a little bit from that,' he said. 'It hasn't been a good summer. I haven't enjoyed it.'

'He was very solid, a good putter. I had recognised a tenacity in his make-up. Here was someone who would give everything for the team cause on the course and would be an important, bubbly figure in the team room.'

Sam recognised that Paul's background in team sports would be vital in building a strong team ethic.

'Sam's input at the Belfry was huge. He had a tough job but he handled it well,' said Paul. 'He was dealt a much harder hand than Bernhard Langer (captain at Oakland Hills in 2004) in so far as there were not as many players on form.

'It was a huge difference between first and second place in terms of Ryder Cup points.'

Low on confidence and worried about the state of his game, Paul's spirits were lifted by the support and encouragement of European captain Sam Torrance.

'He took me up to the Belfry a week before the event and we played a round together. All the time he was talking to me about the pairings he was going to use and telling me everything that was going to happen. I was a rookie and I felt he showed me a lot of respect by doing that,' said Paul.

'I knew the role I was going to fill and that it wasn't going to be massive compared to people like Padraig or Darren.'

Regardless of Paul's lack of form, Torrance clearly understood just how valuable the Dubliner could be in the team environment.

'I loved Paul's golf and his attitude', wrote Sam in his autobiography.

'He really had seven players on form; three guys were average and two were way off simply because the event had been delayed by a year. In 2004 all twelve guys were playing well. The Ryder Cup was a few weeks after the final qualifying event and everyone was on form.'

Paul was concerned about his game, but he was also excited at the prospect of making his Ryder Cup debut at the Belfry and determined to acquit himself well.

'It's great to be here,' he said at an early press conference. 'Now that I've achieved getting here, the important thing is to go and play well. I want more than just to be here; I want to go and compete and be part of the game.'

He was ready to go, but the rookie was forced to wait for his debut, sitting out the morning session on day one. Torrance drafted him in for the afternoon foursomes paired with fellow Dubliner, Padraig Harrington, against Jim Furyk and Stewart Cink. The Irish pair never got going and after turning for home two down, they were eventually beaten 2 and 1.

'It was disappointing, but I wasn't deflated by the outcome of the match,' said Paul. 'My realisation was that I was playing with the big boys in the big environment. We played well but we just came up against two guys who played very well. It's a case of understanding that we had come up against a brick wall and there was nothing else to do but move on.'

The Americans fought back that afternoon following a poor display in the fourballs and by the end of day one Europe had a narrow 4½-3½ lead.

Paul again sat out the morning session on day two, returning to the fray in the afternoon to partner another Irishman, Darren Clarke, in the final fourball match. With Europe slowly losing their advantage as the afternoon wore on, Paul's match against Furyk and Scott Hoch took on huge importance.

Europe needed at least a half to go into the singles all square at eight points apiece, but that looked unlikely with the Americans leading by two with five to play. Clarke got the Irish pair back on track with a chip-in birdie from the fringe at the 14th and then Paul levelled the match by hitting a wedge to three feet at the 16th for a winning birdie.

on a hunch from Bernhard Langer, encouraged Paul to play out of turn.

'Sam came over to me, whacked me on the backside and whispered, "I fancy you going first here. Are you happy about that?"' said Paul.

'I was 40 yards ahead of Darren and ended up hitting first. That was all due to Langer and that was arguably the most crucial thing that happened all week.'

From the middle of the fairway, the rookie fired a long iron into the heart of the green. The Americans failed to find the green in two and missed out on par, giving Paul two putts for a priceless half.

'It was a big half-point for the team and I was happy to play a part in it,' said Paul. 'We got back to the team room and were high fiving each other, even though it was only Saturday night. The half we made meant we hadn't lost any momentum.'

Torrance, sensing the mood of his team and conscious of the need for a fast start in the singles, then took a gamble by putting his best players out early in the 12 singles matches.

> 'My realisation was that I was playing with the big boys in the big environment.'

The momentum appeared to be swinging back in favour of the Europeans, but at the par five 17th Hoch holed from 12 feet to put the Americans back in front with one to play. All four players cleared the water at the 18th, but Clarke and Hoch found the rough off the tee while Paul and Furyk were in prime position in the middle of the fairway.

With Clarke preparing to play first, Torrance, working

By the time Colin Montgomerie brushed aside Scott Hoch 5 and 4 in the opening match the Europeans were clearly in the ascendancy and the rest of the team were swept along, with Paul finally putting the finishing touches to a superb European victory.

Langer's vital intervention in the Clarke/McGinley fourball match that Saturday at the Belfry was indicative of the intuitive and methodical approach he brought to

Paul McGinley hits a shot during practice ahead of the Ryder Cup at the Belfry (September 2002).

his captaincy of the European team at Oakland Hills.

'Both Bernhard and Sam were actually very similar in their approach. They were both very well organised and gave us a lot of confidence,' said Paul. 'Bernhard was dealt a better hand than Sam, but that doesn't necessarily mean you're going to win a Ryder Cup. You're still going to need a strong captain, and Bernhard certainly filled that role.

'At the end of the day the captain is important but it is the players who go out and do it. The captain puts the pairings together and then lets them off; that's what it boils down to. He has a huge role, but when you get on to the course it's just you, your partner and your caddies.'

As at the Belfry two years previously, the European team featured the Irish triumvirate of Paul, Darren Clarke and Padraig Harrington.

'I think it's wonderful that for a second year in a row we have three Irishmen on the team,' Paul stated at the time. 'Personally, I'm very proud of that.'

Full of confidence after playing so well to qualify, Paul expressed a wish to take on a more senior role in a team which featured five rookies.

Paul McGinley (*right*) looks on as Tiger Woods lines up a putt during the Ryder Cup at Oakland Hills, Michigan, USA (September 2004).

'I would like to think of myself as a more senior player than an in-between player,' he explained. 'I know I've only played one Ryder Cup, but my experiences were enough for two or three or maybe ten Ryder Cups put together.'

'I'm one of seven who have played before and I certainly learned a lot the last time, which I will be sharing with the rest of the team, particularly the rookies.'

Langer clearly heeded Paul's words and when the draw came out for the opening morning fourballs (a series that included all three Irishmen), he was paired with the young English rookie, Luke Donald.

Facing Stewart Cink and Chris Riley, the Europeans took a one-hole lead at the 6th when Paul sank in a putt from 13 feet. The Dubliner then sank a 25-footer on the 7th to cancel out a longer effort from Cink to maintain their slender lead.

A tap-in from Riley at the 8th left the match all square, which is how it stayed until the 13th, when a two-putt par from Paul edged Europe ahead again. A great birdie by Cink at the 15th brought the sides level and despite a superb long iron at the last by Donald which found the putting surface, Riley holed a brave seven foot putt to halve the match.

'Bernhard told me that he felt he needed somebody with a little bit of experience to play with Luke, to guide him through his first match, and hopefully I provided that for him,' said Paul.

'It was a tight game all the way round and there was never more than a hole in it. I am very proud of what Luke did on the 18th. Tom Watson did that at Birkdale, hit a two-iron and said it was the greatest shot he had ever hit, and you won't get much more pressure than the last hole of a Ryder Cup. I'm proud of him. He is a great partner.'

It turned out to be a spectacular morning for Europe winning 3½ points and then the team followed that up with another excellent display in the afternoon foursomes to take a record 6½-1½ lead into day two. Langer, facing the media on Friday evening, tried to put the performance of his team into words.

'To have probably the biggest lead that we've ever had after the first day is just incredible and awesome and fantastic. I'm very proud of my guys,' he said.

Paul was rested during the Saturday morning fourballs as the Americans attempted to hit back following their disastrous showing on day one. The crowd, which had been stunned into silence on Friday, responded to the efforts of the home team as the US claimed 2½ points out of the four on offer. At one stage a clean sweep looked possible but, crucially for Europe, rookies Paul Casey and David Howell stemmed the tide by winning their match on the 18th.

It was a vital moment and Paul was quick to heap praise on the debutants. 'There are two English lads who changed the whole momentum of the morning for us, David Howell and Paul Casey,' he told the press. 'We looked like losing 4-0 this morning at one stage, and to come out of this morning's series of matches with 1½ points in terms of winning the Ryder Cup was massive.'

'To have probably the biggest lead that we've ever had after the first day is just incredible.'

Paul returned to action in the afternoon, partnering Harrington in the final foursome of the day against Tiger Woods and Davis Love. Two down after two holes, the Irish pair settled down and by the time they turned for home they were in control and leading by one. Cheered on by a large and vociferous Irish contingent in the crowd, the two friends knuckled down to their task and blitzed their opponents over the back nine to win 4 and 3.

'There's certainly more atmosphere when you play Woods because he takes such a large crowd with him,' said Paul. 'I enjoyed it. I thrived in the atmosphere around each green and each tee. I loved the intensity of it.'

good talking to going down the 14th. I really wanted to finish by winning my game. I didn't want to drift off and end up losing or halving after being four up at one stage.'

There was never really any chance of that happening, and Cink was soon dispatched 3 and 2 as Europe wrapped up an emphatic 18½-9½ victory.

A short while after the trophy presentation, and with 'Ole, Ole' chants still ringing in the background, Paul was asked about Ireland hosting the Ryder Cup.

'Oh, that's going to be something, isn't it?' he said. 'When you watch it on TV you really — if you're a

> **'There's certainly more atmosphere when you play Woods because he takes such a large crowd with him.'**

The Europeans finished day two with an incredible 11-5 lead. Far from losing ground, they had actually stretched further ahead and the question was not so much whether Europe could win, but by how much. In naming his singles line-up, Langer hedged his bets somewhat by putting Paul out second last with Padraig Harrington out last.

'The idea was that we had such huge Irish support that Bernhard wanted to keep us close together as a way of keeping the Irish support going,' said Paul. 'He also wanted to keep two guys who had been through it before at the end, just in case.'

Paul was already four up on opponent Stewart Cink when he reached the 13th tee and heard that Colin Montgomerie had holed the winning putt for Europe.

'I lost a bit of concentration and three-putted 13 for my first bogey of the day,' he said. 'I gave myself a

player — you really want to be involved in this. And it's a really hard team to make. But let's enjoy this one first. Then we'll look to Ireland.'

Paul McGinley misses a birdie putt on the 5th green during the Ryder Cup foursomes at the Belfry (September 2002).

Appendix 1 Players and Records

Fred Daly played 8, won 3, lost 4, halved 1 (1947/49/51/53)
Harry Bradshaw played 5, won 2, lost 2, halved 1 (1953/55/57)
Christy O'Connor played 36, won 11, lost 21, halved 4 (1955/57/59/61/63/65/67/69/71/73)
Norman Drew played 1, won 0, lost 0, halved 1 (1959)
Jimmy Martin played 1, won 0, lost 1, halved 0 (1965)
Hugh Boyle played 3, won 0, lost 3, halved 0 (1967)
Eddie Polland played 2, won 0, lost 2, halved 0 (1973)
John O'Leary played 4, won 0, lost 4, halved 0 (1975)
Christy O'Connor Jnr played 4, won 1, lost 3, halved 0 (1975/89)
Eamonn Darcy played 11, won 1, lost 8, halved 2 (1975/77/81/87)
Des Smyth played 7, won 2, lost 5, halved 0 (1979/81)
Ronan Rafferty played 3, won 1, lost 2, halved 0 (1989)
David Feherty played 3, won 1, lost 1, halved 1 (1991)
Philip Walton played 2, won 1, lost 1, halved 0 (1995)
Darren Clarke played 17, won 7, lost 7, halved 3 (1997/99/2002/2004)
Padraig Harrington played 12, won 7, lost 4, halved 1 (1999/2002/2004)
Paul McGinley played 6, won 2, lost 1, halved 3 (2002/2004)

Appendix 2 Ryder Cup Teams

2004 team	Captain — Bernhard Langer; C. Montgomerie, I. Poulter, P. Harrington, P. Casey, D. Howell, P. McGinley, D. Clarke, L. Westwood, T. Levet, M. A. Jimenez, L. Donald, S. Garcia
2002 team	Captain — Sam Torrance; C. Montgomerie, S. Garcia, D. Clarke, B. Langer, P. Harrington, T. Bjorn, L. Westwood, N. Fasth, P. McGinley, P. Fulke, P. Price, J. Parnevik
1999 team	Captain — Mark James; L. Westwood, D. Clarke, J. Sandelin, J. Van de Velde, A. Coltart, J. Parnevik, P. Harrington, M. A. Jimenez, J. M. Olazabal, C. Montgomerie, S. Garcia, P. Lawrie
1997 team	Captain — Seve Ballesteros; I. Woosnam, P.-U. Johansson, C. Rocca, T. Bjorn, D. Clarke, J. Parnevik, J. M. Olazabal, B. Langer, L. Westwood, C. Montgomerie, N. Faldo, I. Garrido
1995 team	Captain — Bernard Gallacher; S. Ballesteros, H. Clark, M. James, I. Woosnam, C. Rocca, D. Gilford, C. Montgomerie, N. Faldo, S. Torrance, B. Langer, P. Walton, P.-U. Johansson
1993 team	Captain – Bernard Gallacher; I. Woosnam, B. Lane, C. Montgomerie, P. Baker, J. Haeggman, M. James, C. Rocca, S. Ballesteros, J. M. Olazabal, B. Langer, N. Faldo, S. Torrance
1991 team	Captain – Bernard Gallacher; N. Faldo, D. Feherty, C. Montgomerie, J. M. Olazabal, S. R. Richardson, S. Ballesteros, I. Woosnam, P. Broadhurst, S. Torrance, M. James, B. Langer, D. Gilford
1989 team	Captain – Tony Jacklin; S. Ballesteros, B. Langer, J. M. Olazabal, R. Rafferty, H. Clark, M. James, C. O'Connor Jnr, J. M. Canizares, G. Brand Jnr, S. Torrance, N. Faldo, I. Woosnam
1987 team	Captain – Tony Jacklin; I. Woosnam, H. Clark, S. Torrance, N. Faldo, J. M. Olazabal, J. Rivero, A. Lyle, E. Darcy, B. Langer, S. Ballesteros, K. Brown, G. Brand Jnr
1985 team	Captain – Tony Jacklin; M. Pinero, I. Woosnam, P. Way, S. Ballesteros, A. Lyle, B. Langer, S. Torrance, H. Clark, J. Rivero, N. Faldo, J. M. Canizares, K. Brown
1983 team	Captain – Tony Jacklin; S. Ballesteros, N. Faldo, B. Langer, G. J. Brand, A. Lyle, B. Waites, P. Way, S. Torrance, I. Woosnam, J. M. Canizares, K. Brown, B. Gallacher
1981 team	Captain – John Jacobs; S. Torrance, A. Lyle, B. Gallacher, M. James, D. Smyth, B. Langer, M. Pinero, J. M. Canizares, N. Faldo, H. Clark, P. Oosterhuis, E. Darcy
1979 team	Captain – John Jacobs; A. Garrido, S. Ballesteros, K. Brown, M. James, P. Oosterhuis, N. Faldo, B. Gallacher, B. Barnes, D. Smyth, A. Lyle, M. King, A. Jacklin
1977 team	Captain – Brian Huggett; H. Clark, N. C. Coles, P. Dawson, B. Barnes, T. Horton, B. Gallacher, E. Darcy, M. James, N. Faldo, P. Oosterhuis, A. Jacklin, K. Brown
1975 team	Captain – Bernard J. Hunt; B. Barnes, B. Gallacher, N. Wood, M. Bembridge, A. Jacklin, P. Oosterhuis, T. Horton, J. O'Leary, E. Darcy, C. O'Connor Jnr, G. L. Hunt, B. Huggett

1973 team	Captain – Bernard J. Hunt; B. Barnes, B. Gallacher, P. J. Butler, A. Jacklin, N. C. Coles, C. O'Connor, M. Bembridge, P. Oosterhuis, B. Huggett, B. Gallacher, E. Polland, C. Clark
1971 team	Captain – Eric C. Brown; A. Jacklin, B. Gallacher, B. Barnes, P. Oosterhuis, P. Townsend, C. O'Connor, H. Bannerman, N. C. Coles, B. Huggett, J. Garner, P. J. Butler, M. Bembridge
1969 team	Captain – Eric C. Brown; P. Alliss, P. Townsend, N. C. Coles, B. Barnes, C. O'Connor, M. Bembridge, P. J. Butler, A. Jacklin, B. Gallacher, B. Huggett, G. A. Caygill, B. Hunt
1967 team	Captain – Dai J. Rees; H. Boyle, P. Alliss, A. Jacklin, B. Huggett, N. C. Coles, M. Gregson, D. C. Thomas, B. J. Hunt, C. O'Connor, G. Will
1965 team	Captain – Harry Weetman; J. Hitchcock, L. Platts, P. J. Butler, N. C. Coles, B. J. Hunt, D. C. Thomas, P. Alliss, G. Will, C. O'Connor, J. Martin
1963 team	Captain – John Fallon; G. M. Hunt, B. Huggett, P. Alliss, N. C. Coles, D. Thomas, C. O'Connor, H. Weetman, B. J. Hunt, T. B. Haliburton, G. Will
1961 team	Captain – Dai J. Rees; H. Weetman, P. Alliss, B. J. Hunt, T. B. Haliburton, J. Panton, K. Bousfield, N. C. Coles, C. O'Connor, R. L. Moffitt
1959 team	Captain – Dai J. Rees; B. J. Hunt, E. C. Brown, D. J. Rees, K. Bousfield, C. O'Connor, P. Alliss, H. Weetman, D. C. Thomas, N. Drew, R. P. Mills
1957 team	Captain – Dai J. Rees; P. Alliss, B. J. Hunt, K. Bousfield, D. J. Rees, M. Faulkner, H. Weetman, C. O'Connor, E. C. Brown, R. P. Mills, H. Bradshaw
1955 team	Captain – Dai J. Rees; C. O'Connor, H. Bradshaw, J. Fallon, J. R. M. Jacobs, E. C. Brown, S. Scott, A. Lees, H. Weetman, D. J. Rees, K. Bousfield
1953 team	Captain – Henry Cotton; H. Weetman, P. Alliss, E. C. Brown, J. Panton, J. Adams, B. J. Hunt, F. Daly, H. Bradshaw, D. J. Rees, M. Faulkner
1951 team	Captain – Arthur J. Lacey; M. Faulkner, D. J. Rees, C. H. Ward, A. Lees, J. Adams, J. Panton, F. Daly, K. Bousfield, H. Weetman, J. Hargreaves
1949 team	Captain – Charlie Whitcombe; M. Faulkner, J. Adams, F. Daly, K. Bousfield, C. H. Ward, S. L. King, R. Burton, A. Lees, D. J. Rees, L. Ayton
1947 team	Captain – Henry Cotton; F. Daly, J. Adams, M. Faulkner, C. H. Ward, A. Lees, T. H. Cotton, D. J. Rees, S. L. King, E. Greene, R. Horne

Select Bibliography

Concannon , Dale, *The Ryder Cup – The Complete History of Golf's Greatest Drama,* Aurum Press 2001.

Dabell, Norman, *How We Won the Ryder Cup — The Caddies' Stories,* Mainstream 1998.

Gallacher, Bernard, *Captain at Kiawah,* Chapman 1991.

Gilleece, Dermot, *The Brad – The Life and Times of Harry Bradshaw,* audiotapes and book (n.d.).

Hamer, Malcolm, *The Ryder Cup – The Players,* Kingswood 1992.

Harman, Colin, *The Ryder Cup — The Definitive History of Playing Golf for Pride and Country,* McGraw-Hill/Contemporary 1999.

Hobbs, Michael, *The Ryder Cup – The Illustrated History,* MacDonald and Co. 1989.

James, Mark, *Into the Bear Pit,* Virgin Publishing 2000.

Redmond, John and Christy O'Connor, *Christy O'Connor — his Autobiography,* Gill & Macmillan 1985.

Smith, Seamus, *Himself — Christy O'Connor,* Colorman (n.d.).

Torrance, Sam, *Sam: The Autobiography of Sam Torrance,* BBC 2003.

INDEX

Adamson, Tony, 9, 128
AGFA Colour Golf Match, 100
AIB Irish Seniors Open, 154
Alcan Golfer of the Year
    Tournament, 46
Alexander, Skip, 17
Alfred Dunhill Open, 198
Alliss, Peter, 8, 13, 21, 28, 32, 63,
    66, 69, 70, 83, 84
    pairing with Christy O'Connor,
    45–9
Armagh, 53
Assistant Professionals
    Tournament, 74, 88
Austrian Open, 168
Azinger, Paul, 163, 178, 204

Bacon, Sam, 53
Ballesteros, Seve, 123, 125, 127,
    133, 151, 153–4, 163, 177, 178,
    89, 190, 193, 201, 227
Ballybunion, 192
Balmoral Golf Club (Belfast), 13,
    52, 91, 94, 175
Bangor Golf Club, 174
Bannerman, Harry, 98
Barclays Classic, 215
Barnes, Brian, 110, 112, 114, 153,
    174
Beard, Frank, 39, 49
Beck, Chip, 163, 178
Belfry, 9, 118, 121, 128, 159–60,
    162, 194–6, 202, 205, 214, 216,
    217, 222–5, 227, 231, 235
Bell's Scottish Open, 177
Belvoir Park Golf Club, 94
Bembridge, Maurice, 98–100
Bennett, Howard, 212
Benson and Hedges Tournament,
    97
Berkshire Golf Club, 50, 79
Birkdale, 8, 9, 21, 38, 39, 40, 44,
    47–9, 65, 68, 106
Bjorn, Thomas, 7, 204–5
Blancas, Homero, 98
BMW International, 209, 225–6
Bolt, Tommy 'Thunder', 42–3
Boros, Julius, 33, 71–2, 87
Bousfield, Ken, 17, 34, 35, 55, 80,
    175
Boyle, Hugh, 76–89, 236
    career, 76–89
    Ryder Cup (1967), 77, 81–9
Bradshaw, Harry, 8, 22–35, 37, 236
    career, 22–35
    Ryder Cup (1953), 19–20, 27,
    30–32
    Ryder Cup (1955), 32–3, 42
    Ryder Cup (1957), 33–5, 37, 38,
    40, 54
Bradshaw, Jimmy, 137
Bradshaw, Ned, 25
Bramley Golf Club, 66
Brand, Gordon, Jnr, 165, 215
Brewer, Gay, 89
British Match Play

Championship, 13–14
Broadhurst, Paul, 142
Bromford-Adgey Cup, 27
Brookline, 197, 199, 203–4, 206,
    209, 215–17, 221
Brown, Eric, 32, 35, 55
Brown, Ken, 123, 133, 145, 147,
    151, 152
Bruen, Jimmy, 8, 11
Buckinghamshire Golf Club, 115
Bundoran Golf Club, 41–2, 45
Burke, Jack, 32, 33
Burke, Jack, Jnr, 98, 101
Burkemo, Walter, 19–20, 31
Burton, Dick, 79–80
Bush, George, 163
Butler, Peter, 69, 71, 80
Byrne, Matthew, 127

Calcavecchia, Mark, 124, 125,
    159, 160–61, 164, 166, 167–8,
    173, 218–19
Canada Cup, 25, 33, 69, 72, 78, 89
Canizares, José Maria, 125, 128,
    155
Carlow, 119
Carr, Joe, 8, 11
Carroll, Don, 112
Carroll's International
    Tournament, 68, 75
Carroll's Irish Open, 105, 108, 112,
    120, 124
Carroll's Match Play, 119, 120
Castlerock Golf Club, 144
Catalan Open, 177, 186
Celtic Manor Resort Wales Open,
    228
Cink, Stewart, 221, 229, 233, 234
City of Derry Club, 13
Clark, Clive, 98, 100–101
Clark, Eddie, 98
Clark, Howard, 163, 164
Clarke, Darren, 187, 188, 189,
    194–207, 236
    career, 194–207
    Ryder Cup (1997), 201–3
    Ryder Cup (1999), 195, 197, 199,
    203–4, 206
    Ryder Cup (2002), 204–5
    Ryder Cup (2004), 195–7, 198,
    205–7, 230, 232
Club de Campo, 215
Coles, Neil, 49, 69, 80, 84, 89, 115
Collinge, Tom, 79
Coombe Hill Golf Club, 74, 79–80,
    88
Cotton, Henry, 14, 18, 19, 30, 32,
    175
County Armagh Golf Club, 53
County Down Golf Club, 37, 90,
    93
County Sligo Golf Club, 215
Couples, Fred, 117, 118, 121, 127–8,
    163, 168, 177, 190, 201–2
Credit Lyonnais, 177
Crenshaw, Ben, 131, 133–4, 141,

155–7, 193
Crosby, Bob, 60

Dabel, Norman, 164
Daks Tournament, 47, 80
Dalmahoy, 80
Daly, Fred, 8, 10–21, 28, 52, 54,
    94–5, 97, 161, 175, 236
    career, 10–21
    Ryder Cup (1947), 14–17
    Ryder Cup (1949), 17
    Ryder Cup (1951), 18
    Ryder Cup (1953), 10, 18–21, 25,
    27, 28, 30–32
Darcy, Eamonn, 130–43, 197, 236
    career, 130–43
    Ryder Cup (1975), 109, 110, 114,
    120, 138–9
    Ryder Cup (1977), 139–41
    Ryder Cup (1981), 141
    Ryder Cup (1987), 131–6, 139,
    141–2, 177, 212
Darcy, Jack, 137
Darcy, Martin, 137
Darwin, Bernard, 25
Delgany Golf Club, 25, 26–7,
    136–7
Demaret, Jimmy, 18
Denham, 115
de Vicenzo, Roberto, 80
Dickinson, Gardner, 84
Dobereiner, Peter, 147, 149
Donald, Luke, 233
Down, County, 37, 90, 93
Doyle, Pat, 136
Drew, Norman, 45, 50–63, 236
    career, 50–63
    Ryder Cup (1959), 51, 52–63
Druids Glen, 130
Dryden, Stuart, 164, 167
Dubai Desert Classic, 140
Dublin, 42, 119, 212
Dunbar Open, 30
Dungannon Golf Club, 197
Dunhill Cup, 152, 161, 175, 177,
    189
Dunhill British Masters, 118, 123
Dun Laoghaire Golf Club, 105
Dunlop Masters, 32, 34
Durnian, Denis, 123
Duval, David, 198, 203, 205
Dye, Pete, 177

East of Ireland Championship, 53
Edgbaston Golf Club, 79
Edmondstown Golf Club, 66
Eisenhower Trophy, 189
Eldorado Country Club, 45, 52,
    59, 60
Epson Grand Prix of Europe, 175
Erewash Valley Golf Club, 137
Esso Tournament, 69
European Amateur Team Golf
    Championship, 105, 152
European Match Play, 151–2
European Ryder Cup Team
    photos
    1987, 136, 139

1989, 125, 166
1995, 188
2002, 228
European Tour, 115, 125, 161, 168,
    175, 186, 200–201, 215, 226–7

Faldo, Nick, 123, 125, 133, 154,
    162, 163, 177, 180, 189, 192,
    193, 198
Fallon, John, 33
Faulkner, Max, 28, 34, 56
Faxon, Brad, 190
Feherty, David, 170–81, 189, 212,
    236
    career, 170–81
    Ryder Cup (1991), 171–3, 176,
    177–81
Ferguson, M., 56
Finsterwald, Dow, 37–40
Floyd, Raymond, 125, 138, 141,
    155, 163, 166, 177, 180
Ford, Doug, 45, 51, 52, 54, 59, 60
Fota Island Golf Club, 156
Foxrock Golf Club, 105
Furyk, Jim, 205, 223, 225, 229–30

Gallacher, Bernard, 101, 141, 142,
    155
    captaincy, 173, 177–8, 180, 184,
    185, 188, 189, 190–92, 193
Gallacher, Des, 155
Galway Golf Club, 41, 119
Ganton, 17
Garcia, Sergio, 205
Garrido, Antonio, 151
GB & I (Great Britain & Ireland)
    Team photos
    1947, 16
    1953, 27
    1959, 52, 55
    1965, 40, 68
    1969, 9, 44
Geiberger, Al, 138
German Open, 187
Gilford, David, 142, 177, 192
Gilleece, Dermot, 25, 166
Gleeson, Father, 25–7
Gleneagles, 42, 54–5
Gor-Ray Cup Assistants Golf
    Championships, 58
Graham, Lou, 98, 101, 120
Grange Golf Club, 137
Green, Hubert, 140
Green, Ken, 125, 163, 164, 166, 167
Greenbrier, 147
Gregson, Malcolm, 83, 84
Greystones Golf Club, 66
Grubb, Tony, 80

Haas, Fred, 32
Haas, Jay, 183, 185–6, 221
Haliburton, Tom, 47
Hamilton, Bob, 17
Harrington, Paddy, 213
Harrington, Padraig, 53, 148, 197,
    208–21, 227, 236
    career, 208–21
    Ryder Cup (1999), 209–11, 215–17

Ryder Cup (2002), 214, 217, 218–19, 228
Ryder Cup (2004), 7, 9, 208, 210, 213, 219–21, 229, 232, 234
Harrington, Tadhg, 215
Harris, Phil, 43
Harrison, Dutch, 14
Hawkins, Fred, 34
Heafner, Clayton, 18
Hennessey Cognac Cup, 101
Herbert, Lionel, 35
Heritage Golf & Country Club, 154
Hill, Dave, 139
Hitchcock, Jimmy, 55, 69, 71–2
Hoch, Scott, 199, 205, 230
Hogan, Ben, 14, 17, 18, 33, 77, 78, 83, 84, 87
Hohe Brucke Open, 227
Home Internationals, 105, 152
Honda Classic, 215
Horton, Tommy, 110, 113
Houston, 77, 81
Howell, David, 233
Hoylake, 12, 13, 19, 80
Hudson, Robert A., 12
Huggett, Brian, 110, 123, 140
Hunt, Bernard, 21, 32, 49, 84, 98, 100, 109, 110, 113, 138
Hunt, Guy, 110, 114, 138
Hutcheon, Bob, 57

ICL International, 175
International Open Golf Tournament, 78
IPGA (Irish Professional Golfers' Association), 41
Irish Amateur Close Championship, 197, 215
Irish Dunlop, 42, 120
Irish Hospitals Trust Tournament, 48, 53, 56
Irish Masters, 52
Irish Match Play, 119, 120
Irish National Championship, 75
Irish Open, 28, 105, 108, 109, 112, 115, 120, 124, 130, 154, 156, 192
Irish PGA Championship, 144, 151
Irish Professional Championship, 28, 37, 52, 186
Irish Professional Golfers Association (IPGA), 41
Irish Stroke Play, 215
Irwin, Hale, 110, 113, 114, 141, 145, 147, 152, 155, 177, 180, 181
Italian Open, 162, 177

Jacklin, Tony, 49, 83, 98, 106, 110, 112, 113, 139–40, 141, 154, 174
captaincy, 117, 122, 123–7, 128, 157, 163–7, 168, 173, 186
Jacklin, Vivienne, 124
Jacobs, John, 33, 80, 105–6, 141, 147–8, 153, 155
Jacobsen, Fredrik, 226
Jabobsen, Peter, 192
James, Mark, 142, 145, 147, 151,

154, 155, 203, 209, 211
January, Don, 139
Jersey European Open, 123
Jimenez, Miguel Angel, 205
Johansson, Per-Ulrik, 189, 191, 192, 193
Johnston, Fred, 75
Jones, David, 138, 174–5

K Club, 9, 148
Kearney, Ken, 215
Kelly, Sean, 153
Kiawah Island, 142, 172, 173, 176, 177, 215, 228
Kilcroney Golf and Country Club, 27
Kilkenny, 119
Killarney, 42
Killenard, 154
King, Michael, 147–8
Kinsella, Jimmy, 106, 119, 138
Kite, Tom, 145, 147, 163
Kittansett Club, 53
Knock Golf Club, 53
Knockanally, 137
Kobayashi, Yosaji, 78
Kroll, Ted, 15, 18, 32

La Costa Resort and Spa, 198
Lahinch, 93
Langer, Bernhard, 105, 124, 125, 127, 154, 163–4, 166, 181, 189, 192, 193
captaincy, 7, 221, 229, 230–32, 233, 234
Latchford, Ray, 154
Laurel Valley, 103, 120, 138
Laytown and Bettystown Golf Club, 152
Lees, Arthur, 66
Lehman, Tom, 190, 193, 204
Lema, Tony, 71–2
Leonard, Justin, 204, 217
Leopardstown Race Course, 106
Levi, Wayne, 177
Lietzke, Bruce, 155
Lindrick, 33–5, 37–40, 43, 54
Littler, Gene, 49
Locke, Bobby, 21, 28, 30
'Long Drop club', 45, 57
Longhurst, Henry, 25
Love, Davis, 192, 193, 201–2, 205–6, 221, 234
Lurgan, 13
Lyle, Sandy, 124, 133, 154, 155
Lynch, Nick, 65, 66, 68–9, 71, 72, 75
Lytham St Anne's, 13–14, 26, 139

MacDonald, Keith, 50
McGinley, Mick, 226
McGinley, Paul, 7, 9, 148, 197, 199, 212, 215, 222–35, 236
career, 222–35
Ryder Cup (2002), 205, 222–5, 227, 228, 235
Ryder Cup (2004), 7, 9, 213, 221, 229–34

McLauchlan, Bryan, 185, 193
MacWeeney, Paul, 72
Madrid Open Golf Championship, 179
Maggert, Jeff, 190, 192
Magowan, Jack, 12, 13, 15–17, 18, 21, 161, 164
Mahee Island, 13
Malone Golf Club, 62
Mangrum, Lloyd, 14, 17, 32
Mangrum, Mrs Lloyd, 15
Marian (Massachusetts), 53
Marr, Dave, 49, 71
Martin, James, 66
Martin, Jimmy, 64–75, 137, 236
career, 64–75
Ryder Cup (1965), 40, 65, 68, 69–72
Martini Golf Tournament, 50
Martini International, 120
Match Play Championship, 22, 34
May, Alice, 15
May, Bob, 226
Mayer, Dick, 35, 38
Metz, Dick, 56
Mickelson, Phil, 190, 193, 202, 207, 218, 220, 226
Micklem, Gerald, 13, 17
Middlecroft, Cary, 19–20, 31, 32, 33, 59
Miller, Johnny, 110, 113, 120
Mills, Peter, 34, 55, 59, 60
Mirasol Country Club, 215
Montgomerie, Colin, 173, 177, 187, 192, 196, 201–2, 205, 209, 230, 234
partnership with Harrington, 217, 218, 220–21
Moor Park, 24
Moortown, 69
Mosley Golf Club, 78
Mourne Cup, 68–9
Mourne Golf Club, 93
Muirfield (Scotland), 93, 95, 96, 98, 111, 150
Muirfield Village (Ohio), 131, 132, 136
Munich, 225–6
Murdock, Ian, 93
Murphy, Bob, 110
Murphy, Mick, 138
Murphy's Irish Open, 130, 156, 192

Naas, 226
Nathan, Selwyn, 106
Nelson, Byron, 71
News of the World Championship, 82
News of the World Match Play, 55
Newton, Jack, 106
New Zealand Open, 161
Nicklaus, Jack, 49, 69–71, 83, 91–3, 98–9, 100–101, 110, 114, 135, 141, 174
NM English Open, 123
North of Ireland Championship, 53, 197

Nottingham, 97

Oak Hill, 9, 182–6, 190
Oakland Hills, 7, 195–6, 198, 205–6, 208, 210, 213, 219–20, 232
O'Connor, Ann, 122, 123, 127, 128
O'Connor, Christy (Junior), 116–29, 138, 197, 212, 236
career, 116–29
Ryder Cup (1975), 109, 110, 113–14, 120–21, 138
Ryder Cup (1989), 116–18, 121, 122, 123–9, 162, 163, 164–6, 167, 168, 186
O'Connor, Christy (Senior), 8, 25, 33, 68, 69, 89, 118–19, 127, 138, 212
career, 36–49, 236
Ryder Cup (1955), 32, 42–3
Ryder Cup (1957), 34, 35, 37–40, 43, 54
Ryder Cup (1959), 45–6, 52, 55, 59
Ryder Cup (1965), 38, 40, 68, 69
Ryder Cup (1967), 83, 84
Ryder Cup (1969), 9, 39, 44, 49, 109
Ryder Cup (1973), 49, 98
O'Connor, Eugene, 119
O'Connor, Frank, 119
O'Connor, Sean, 119
Oki Pro-Am, 227
Olazabal, José Maria, 162, 163, 177, 178, 189, 204, 209
O'Leary, John, 102–15, 236
career, 102–15
Ryder Cup (1975), 103, 109–14, 120–21, 138
Olton Golf Club, 78, 79
O'Meara, Mark, 178, 211
Oosterhuis, Peter, 113, 151, 154, 174
Open Championship
Bradshaw, Harry, 26, 28–30, 31
Clarke, Darren, 198
Daly, Fred, 12, 19
Darcy, Eamonn, 143
Feherty, David, 170, 180
O'Connor, Christy (Junior), 123, 126
O'Connor, Christy (Senior), 41, 42
O'Leary, John, 111
Polland, Eddie, 90, 97
Rafferty, Ronan, 158
Smyth, Des, 150

Palm Springs, 32–3, 42, 45, 52, 57
Palmer, Arnold, 49, 71, 84, 87, 89, 98–9, 101, 110, 174
Parmeco Classic, 97
Parsonage, David, 137
Pate, Steve, 177
Pavin, Corey, 177, 193
Penfold-Bournemouth Tournament, 97
Peugeot Open de France, 189
PGA (Professional Golfers

Association), 109–10, 123
PGA Championship, 80–81, 215
Piccadilly Tournament, 66–8
Pinehurst, 18, 120
Platts, Lionel, 69, 71, 72
Player, Gary, 56, 106
Polland, Eddie, 90–101, 175, 236
   career, 90–101
   Ryder Cup (1973), 92–3, 95–6,
      97–101
Polland, John, 93
Polland, Robert, 93
Polland, Willie, 93
Portland Golf Club, 14–15
Portmarnock, 30, 52, 105, 226
Portrush, 12–13, 28, 41, 126
Potts, Johnny, 71
Price, Nick, 151
Pro-Am, 91–2, 227

Queen Elizabeth, 55–6
Queen Mary, 16

Rafferty, Ronan, 53, 158–69, 236
   career, 158–69
   Ryder Cup (1989), 125–7, 159–
      61, 162, 163–9
Ralston, 63
Redmond, John, 38
Rees, Dai, 32–3, 34–5, 42, 54, 56,
   57, 59–60, 69, 83, 84, 87, 97
Richardson, Matthew, 115
Richardson, Steven, 177
Riley, Chris, 233
Rivero, José, 123
Roberts, Loren, 190, 192
Robinson, Billy, 94
Rocca, Costantino, 192, 193
Rodriguez, Chi Chi, 98
Rogers, Bill, 155
Royal Birkdale Golf Club, 8, 9, 21,
   38, 39, 40, 44, 47–9, 65, 68, 106
Royal County Down Golf Club,
   37, 90, 93
Royal Dublin, 42, 119, 212
Royal Liverpool, 28
Royal Lytham and St Anne's,
   13–14, 26, 139
Royal Portrush, 12–13, 28, 41, 126
Royal St George's, 28–30, 31, 123
Royal Wimbledon Golf Club,
   66, 89
Royal Zoute Golf Club, 198
Rush Golf Club, 66, 75
Ryder, Samuel, 7
Ryder Cup, 7–9
   statistics of Irish golfers, 236
   1947, 14–17
   1949, 17
   1951, 18
   1953, 10, 18–21, 25, 27, 30–32
   1955, 32–3, 42–3
   1957, 33–5, 37–40, 43, 54
   1959, 45–6, 51, 52–63
   1961, 63
   1965, 8, 40, 65, 68, 69–72
   1967, 77, 81–9
   1969, 44, 49, 106, 174

1973, 49, 92–3, 95–6, 97–101, 110
1975, 103, 109–14, 120–21, 138–9
1977, 123, 139–41
1979, 145, 147–8, 149, 151, 152
1981, 141, 146, 149, 153–7
1985, 123
1987, 131–6, 139, 141–2, 212
1989, 116–18, 121, 122, 123–9,
   159–61, 162, 163–8
1991, 142, 171–3, 176, 177–81
1993, 181
1995, 9, 183–6, 189–93
1997, 201–3
1999, 195, 197, 199, 203–4, 206,
   209–11, 215–17
2001 (postponed), 204, 228
2002, 173–4, 194, 196, 200, 204–5,
   214, 217, 218–19, 222–5,
   227, 228, 235
2004, 7, 9, 195–7, 198, 205–7, 208,
   210, 213, 219–21, 229–34

St Andrews, 20, 42, 46, 118, 158–9,
   161, 177, 180
St Pierre Golf Club, 175
Sanders, Doug, 89, 225
Sandown Park, 80
Sandwich, 28–30, 31
Sarazen, Gene, 21
Scandinavian Masters, 177
Scandinavian Open, 162
Schofield, Ken, 115
Scottish Open, 177
Senior British Open
   Championship, 90
Shandon Park Golf Club, 68
Shearer, Bob, 106
Sherwood Forest, 55
Silent Night Tournament, 68, 69
Silver King Tournament, 24
Sligo, 215
Slough, 100
Smith, Seamus, 45
Smurfit Irish PGA Championship,
   144
Smyth, Des, 144–57, 236
   career, 144–57
   Ryder Cup (1979), 145, 147–8,
      149, 151, 152
   Ryder Cup (1981), 146, 149,
      153–7
Snead, J. C., 49, 110, 113
Snead, Sam, 13, 14, 17, 32, 33, 59,
   60, 78
Sneed, Ed, 139
South Africa Sunshine Tour, 95–7,
   175
South African Masters, 106
South of Ireland crown, 197
South Shields, 119
Spanish Open Championship, 99,
   123, 215
Stackstown Golf Club, 213
Stanley, Ian, 106
Stewart, Payne, 125, 160, 171, 173,
   180–81
Stockton, Dave, 139–40, 177
Strange, Curtis, 124, 163, 190

Struver, Sven, 187
Sullivan, Walter, 137
Sun Alliance European Match
   Play, 151–2
Sun Alliance PGA Match Play, 101
Sunningdale Golf Club, 66
Sunshine Tour (South Africa),
   95–7, 175
Sutton, Hal, 204
Sutton, Norman, 28
Sutton Golf Club, 66
Swallow-Penfold Tournament, 42,
   64, 70, 86

Thomas, Dave, 55, 59, 69, 83
Thomas, Pat Ward, 11, 35
Thunderbird Ranch and Country
   Club, 32, 42
Tokyo, 78, 80, 81
Toms, David, 218
Torrance, Bob, 212, 218
Torrance, Sam, 114, 142, 154,
   173–4, 178–80, 190, 192, 212
   captaincy, 186, 204–5, 218, 225,
      229, 230, 232
Toski, Bob, 106
Townsend, Peter, 98
Trevino, Lee, 98, 110, 113, 114, 147
Troon, 143
Tuam, 41
Turnberry, 170

Ulster Championship, 42

Valderrama, 199, 201–3, 207
Van Donck, Flory, 28
Venezuelan Open, 161
Volvo Masters, 168
Volvo PGA Championship, 123

Wadkins, Lanny, 125, 163, 178,
   180, 190
Walker Cup, 53, 105, 161, 189,
   212, 226
Wall, Art, 34, 45
Wallace, Bob, 41
Wallace, Kevin, 119
Walton, Philip, 9, 142, 163, 182–93,
   197, 212, 236
   career, 182–93
   Ryder Cup (1995), 182–6, 189–93
Walton Heath, 22, 34, 82, 141, 146,
   149, 153
Ward, Charlie, 14
Ward, Mrs Charlie, 15
Warrenpoint Golf Club, 161
Watson, Tom, 125, 163, 233
Weetman, Harry, 32, 34–5, 59, 69,
   70, 72
Weiskopf, Tom, 49, 98, 100–101,
   110, 113–14, 120
Weizmuller, Johnny, 60
Wentworth, 10, 18, 27, 30, 47, 80
West of Ireland Championship,
   209, 215
Westwood, Lee, 196, 203–4, 206,
   207
WGC Accenture Match Play

Championship, 198
Whiston, Adam, 105
Whitcombe, Charlie, 17
White, Liam, 226
Will, George, 80–81, 87–8
Wimbledon, 66, 89
Wiseman, David, 80
Woburn, 162
Wood, Norman, 110
Woodbrook, 48, 75, 120
Woods, Tiger, 198, 200, 201, 203,
   204, 207, 212, 220, 221, 232, 234
Wooler, Rod, 180
Woosnam, Ian, 125, 133, 148, 187,
   188, 189, 190, 192–3, 203
World Cup, 101, 106, 215, 227–8

Yomiuri Open, 78, 80, 81
Yorkshire Evening News
   Tournament, 80

Zambian Open, 120
Zambian Tour, 138
Zoeller, Fuzzy, 147